ZOOM
The Playing Field of Daryl E. Johnson

Gayle Jones Carter

PEGASUS BOOKS

Copyright © 2020 Gayle Jones Carter
All Rights Reserved

Copyright © 2020 by Gayle Jones Carter

All Rights Reserved. No part of this book may be produced or transmitted in any form or by any means, electronic or mechanical, including photocopying, recording or by an information storage and retrieval system—except by a reviewer who may quote brief passages in a review to be printed in a magazine or newspaper—without permission in writing from the publisher.

Pegasus Books
8165 Valley Green Drive
Sacramento, CA 95823
www.pegasusbooks.net

First Edition: September 2020

Published in North America by Pegasus Books. For information, please contact Pegasus Books c/o Marcus McGee, 8165 Valley Green Drive, Sacramento, CA 95823.

Library of Congress Cataloguing-In-Publication Data
Gayle Jones Carter
Zoom/Gayle Jones Carter 1st ed
p. cm.
Library of Congress Control Number: 2020947167

ISBN – 978-1-941859-82-7

1. SPORTS & RECREATION / Football. 2. SPORTS & RECREATION / Sports Psychology. 3. BIOGRAPHY & AUTOBIOGRAPHY / African American & Black. 4. BIOGRAPHY & AUTOBIOGRAPHY / Sports. 5. SOCIAL SCIENCE / Sociology of Sports. 6. SPORTS & RECREATION / Cultural & Social Aspects.

10 9 8 7 6 5 4 3 2 1

Comments about *Zoom* and requests for additional copies, book club rates and author speaking appearances may be addressed to Gayle Jones Carter or Pegasus Books c/o Marcus McGee, 8165 Valley Green Drive, Sacramento, CA, 95823, or you can send your comments and requests via e-mail to GJCZoom@devorecarter.com.

Printed in the United States of America

Welcome to the "Playing Field" of Daryl E. Johnson

Having conversations with Daryl, a childhood friend and classmate, I rediscovered the inner mechanisms of a man that propelled him onto a stage… becoming a national treasure… a high school, college and professional football *star*. I smiled and cried with joy as he shared his life with me.

Growing up in Richmond, Virginia, Daryl navigated the streets of our *segregated city* riding the back of buses, as we Blacks were forced to do in the late 50s. He had childish thoughts wondering why God had made him so dark, and why he couldn't look like "this one" or "that one." Yes, I gave him all the old clichés about being a *sweet black berry,* and we laughed. He agreed with everything I said, and I could not stop laughing!

Daryl told me he was sprinkled with Holy Water at All Souls Presbyterian Church on Overbrook Road, and so was I. He said his baptism gave him a feeling of being **protected** and the comfort of ***belonging.*** Even though his father was absent from the home, his mother made sure she was an everlasting example of leadership and strength for her sons.

Perhaps the absence of a father gave Daryl his strong intestinal fortitude—the *strength of mind* that enabled him to *face danger*, *endure pain* and *challenge adversity with courage.* Today, Daryl is a family man, living in Massachusetts… dealing with some ailments that resulted from playing a *rough and dangerous* sport. He is happy and says he has never been depressed. Daryl is a man speaking his truths and his convictions to all. He *loves to laugh* and enjoys all genres of music, from *Ave Maria* to LXW's Great God, to R&B to George Benson, to Yuna's *Blank Marquee.* The following photographs and documents are treasures from Daryl's collection. Every aspect of his sporting career—both public and private— are explored and richly reproduced. You will see… Daryl's marquee is far from being blank.

Thank you #23, for sharing your life with me.

Gayle Jones Carter

Dedication

I dedicate this book to my wife, children, family, friends, teachers, coaches, teammates, personal and professional associates who contributed to my life.

I also dedicate this book to any young athlete contemplating a professional career in sports. *Get ready to accomplish the extraordinary. In a world where we are so connected by the Internet and globalization, we are still disconnected on an interpersonal level. I believe sports are helping us bridge the gap.*

And to *you,* the reader: E*ven if we have not met*, I'm filled with gratitude because you are looking at my life in pictures. Please know I'm thinking fondly of you.

Daryl E. Johnson

Brandi Johnson

My Dad

Wow, to attempt to put into words how much I love and admire him feels a bit impossible but, I am going to try because one of the many things he has taught me is that "nothing is impossible." One of his famous lines that will forever echo in my mind, "Ain't nothing to it but to do it."

My Daddy (yes, Daddy… still at 38, that's what I call him). He is my rock, a protector. He is intelligent, funny, loving and inspiring. He always speaks his mind, tells the truth and isn't concerned whether that truth is offensive—because he lives by honesty. He has rigorous standards and provides nurturing guidance to everyone who he cares about (doesn't matter if you are blood or not). If he cares, his commitment is obvious. He truly lives by the quote, "We are visitors here on planet Earth, and we are obligated to leave it better than we found it."

Daddy has the ability to make you think, broaden your horizon with questions (even on days when you don't want to think, or you thought you had thought of it all). Dad can and will bring out any individuals nascent motivation. He's the type of motivator who can instill confidence in anyone. He is not only my mentor, as I have witnessed him become a mentor to many.

My father has taught me the importance of humility. "Act like you've scored a touchdown before, Brandi." My success is because of his lessons and love. I strive for greatness because of my dad. He is a true testament of a man who followed a dream in times of racism and adversity, and he didn't let anything get in his way. When I want to give up—I think of him.

"Not all superheroes wear capes." My dad is a superhero.

Foreword
Daryl – The Friend

I remember Daryl when he was still a little boy in elementary school, when he spelled his name "Darryl." As I reflect on the past, I think of him as a beloved friend. If he had been a girl, I would have wanted him to be my "BFF." Why? Because Daryl would always have your back. You could trust him, depend on him and enjoy his company because he was bright and fun to be with. He was not like the other overzealous teenage boys—out to "claim a girlfriend(s)."

He respected females and seemed immune to the attention he received as fickle teenage girls wanted to be noticed by him, the school's most popular athlete. More importantly, boys wanted to claim Daryl as their friend too. He was "the man." But Daryl didn't think of himself that way. He was humble, not boastful, and rather serious for his age. He was going to be competitive in any sport, but football was his forte. He seemed to want to always do better, push harder, never resting on his laurels.

During those dark days of segregation, the Richmond population had at least one major event to look forward to—the annual Armstrong-Walker game. Records show that crowds of at least 30,000 came to that game every year, and we MLW fans needed our heroes to give us city bragging rights. Daryl was one of our greatest heroes. I have no idea if Daryl ever had butterflies about the games, but we had tremendous confidence in him, and he never let us down. He was resilient, athletic, and had EVERYTHING it took to help take us to a win, game after game.

The Armstrong-Walker game was the city's battle for pride. In our senior year, our amazing football team won that special game, 21 to 7. Our opponents that year scored a total of 39 points against us while our team had scored a total of 194 points. With scores like that, we were certainly not a one-man-show, but we had an amazing team! I have no doubt being a part of this team and being such a valuable contributor was very important to Daryl, or DeeJay, as he was called.

I know Daryl was amazing as an athlete, and that's what most of our old classmates bring up over and over. But Daryl, *the person*, was what really made him so very special. To be so outstanding athletically and stay grounded as a teenager was special in itself. But if you were Daryl's friend, he made YOU feel special. He was always warm and kind and complimentary to you rather than a person wanting to be complimented.

I did well academically and never needed any help in my classes. But one day in my class in trigonometry I was stumped by a problem. We could mingle to get the answer, and Daryl came over to me and solved the problem in no time! I always knew he was smart, but had I forgotten about it, as he was admired for his physical prowess, not his intellect. That very day, I never thought of my friend as the athlete anymore. To me he was Daryl, the intellect, Daryl the consummate friend who was humble and giving and caring.

He was the friend in need, the friend to be proud of, the friend you wanted to be with who could make you happy in his presence and who could make you feel special and respected. All of us who knew Daryl, the athlete, were blessed to also have such an amazing friend who inspired us, because of his character, his drive to be the best he could be, his capabilities and his love for his family and close friends.

**Dr. Carolyn Branch Brooks,
Maggie L. Walker Class of 1964**

1st Quarter — My Life in Richmond, VA   **page 1**

Albert V. Norrell Elementary
Benjamin A. Graves Jr. High
Maggie L. Walker High School

2nd Quarter — College   **page 21**
Records Set at Morgan State
Tangerine Bowl
Player of the Year – Small Colleges 1967

3rd Quarter — NFL and the Boston Patriots   **page 43**
The Pros
Stepping onto a Stage Revered by Millions

4th Quarter — No Deposits, No Returns   **page 69**
Family
Art

Overtime — Giving Back/Paying it Forward   **page97**
Letters of Recognition
Race Issues

Health — Personal   **page 121**
Harvard Letter
Baltimore Sun Article

Links   **page 135**
Music and Laughter — The Best Medicine
And the Game Continues…

Richmond, Virginia

1st Quarter

Albert V. Norrell Elementary School

This school was on Richmond's Northside and most friends pictured here continued through elementary school and graduated from Maggie L. Walker in 1964.

Benjamin A. Graves Jr. High School

Class Officers were all good friends.

Maggie L. Walker High School

Classmates gather on the steps of Maggie L. Walker

Senior Picture, Maggie L. Walker High

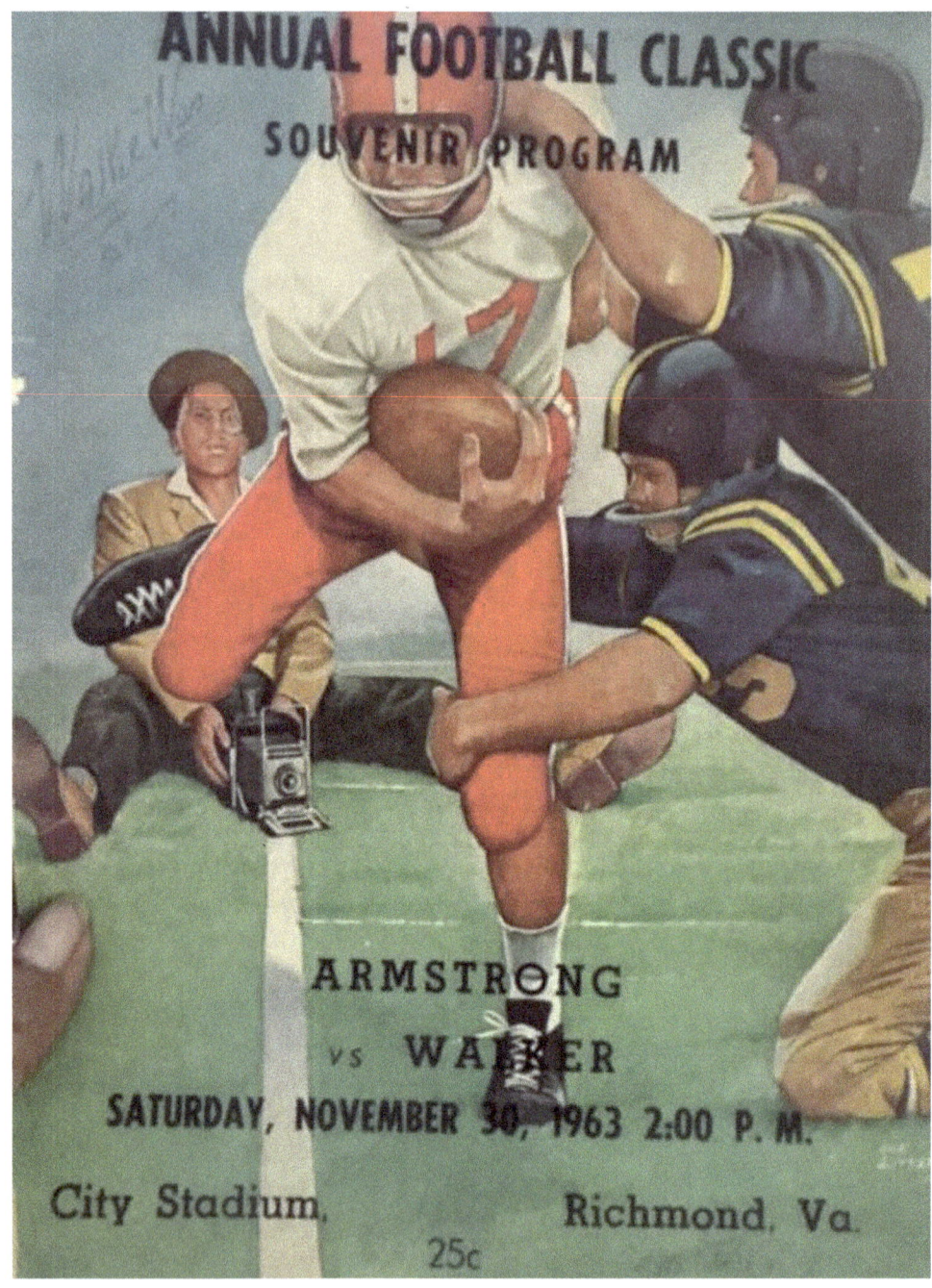

I played my last football game for Maggie L. Walker at City Stadium in Richmond, VA, and my first professional game at the same stadium against Joe Namath and the NY Jets. I could feel the combination of my amateur and professional experience taking place in my life at the same location. It was only five years between the two games.

The Silver Coach

The Silver Coach was across the street from Maggie Walker, where friends met before heading home. I would order a cheeseburger or bologna burger and a root beer soda. I would meet Arnold Stallings, Bucky, Leon Jasper and others, and we would walk home through Brookfield.

Daryl Johnson

When you can play football with a smile, you love the sport. The reason I wore #23 in high school and in the pros was because I always liked Psalm 23. Morgan would not let me wear #23, I did ask for it. I guess it was a way of letting me know that I couldn't have everything I wanted in life.

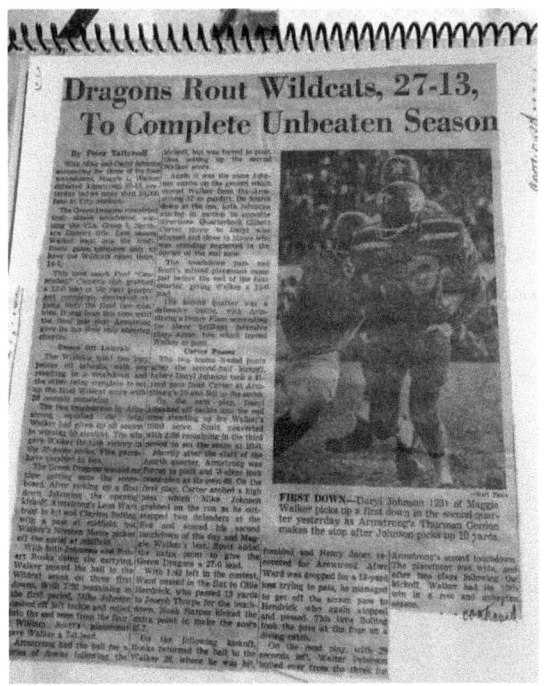

Dragons Rout Wildcats, 27-13, to Complete Unbeaten Season

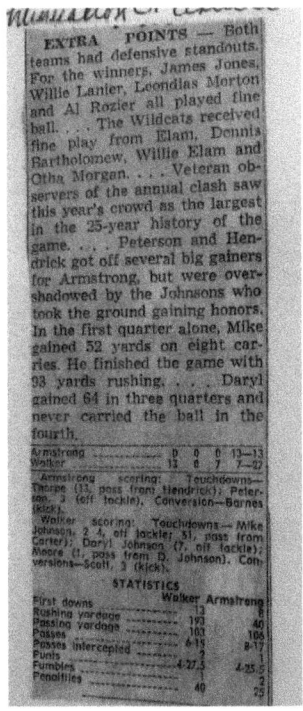

Daryl gained 64 in three quarters and never carried the ball in the fourth

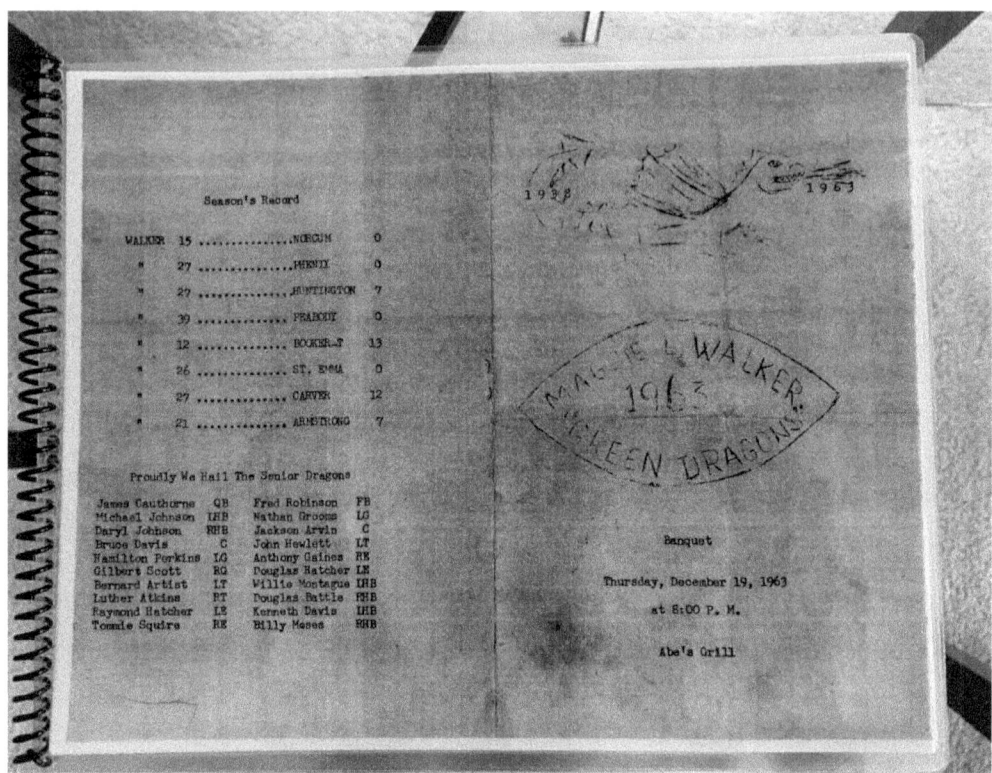

Kermit Foster's sister was a fan. She saved memorabilia and sent them to me a few years ago.

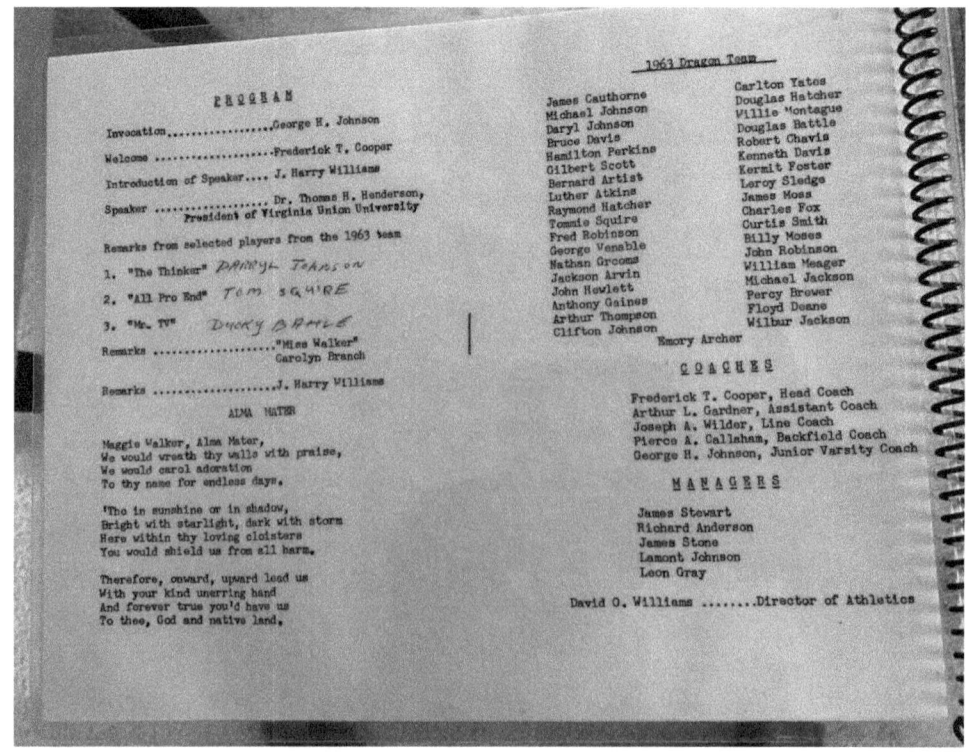

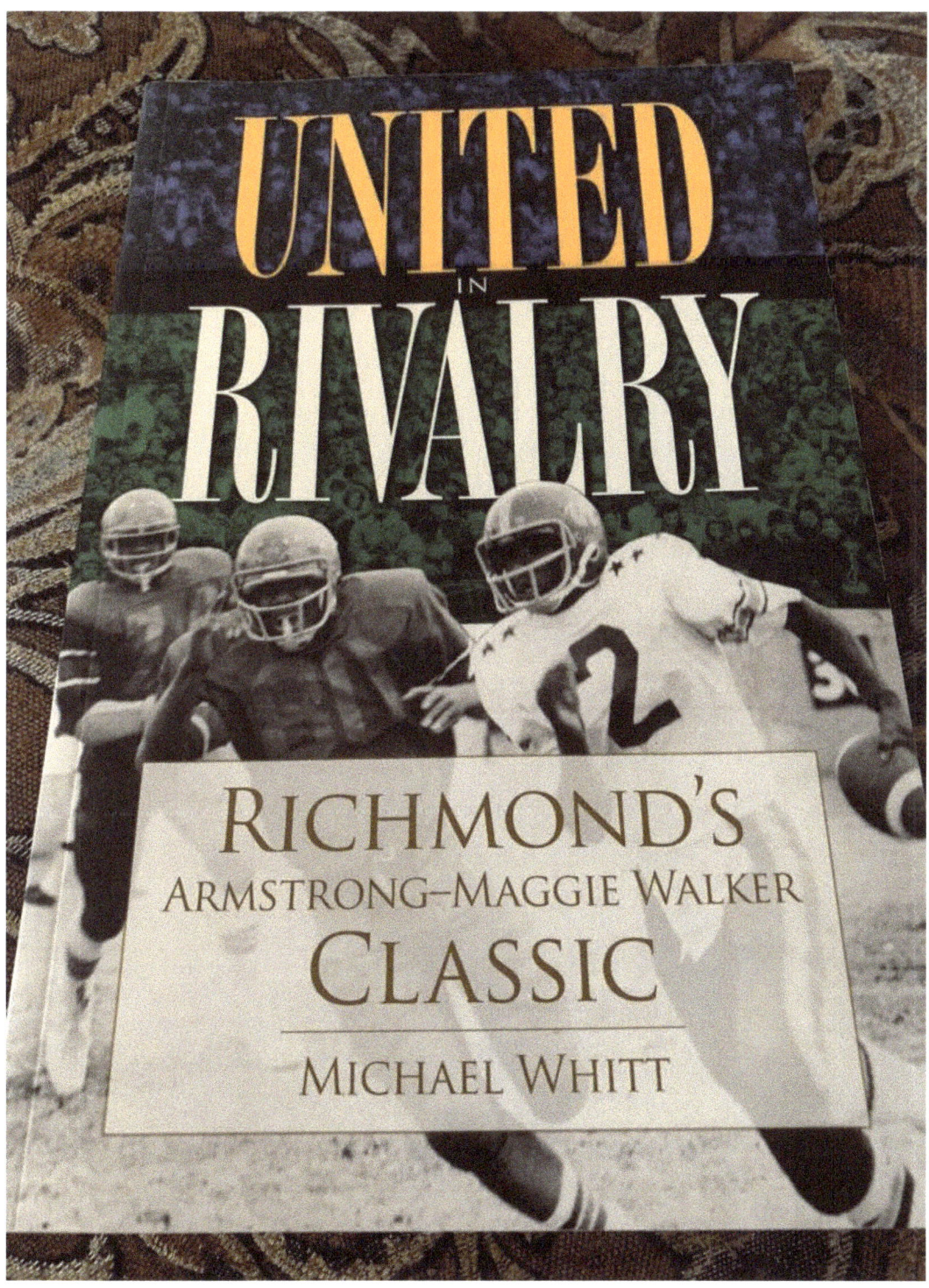

There was nothing more exciting than a Maggie Walker & Armstrong Classic on a sunny fall day in Richmond. The city was draped in green and white and orange and blue.

Daryl #23 Standing

Playing with my teammates and for my classmates at Maggie L. Walker in some of the most memorable days of my life.
(Daryl, #23 front row left)

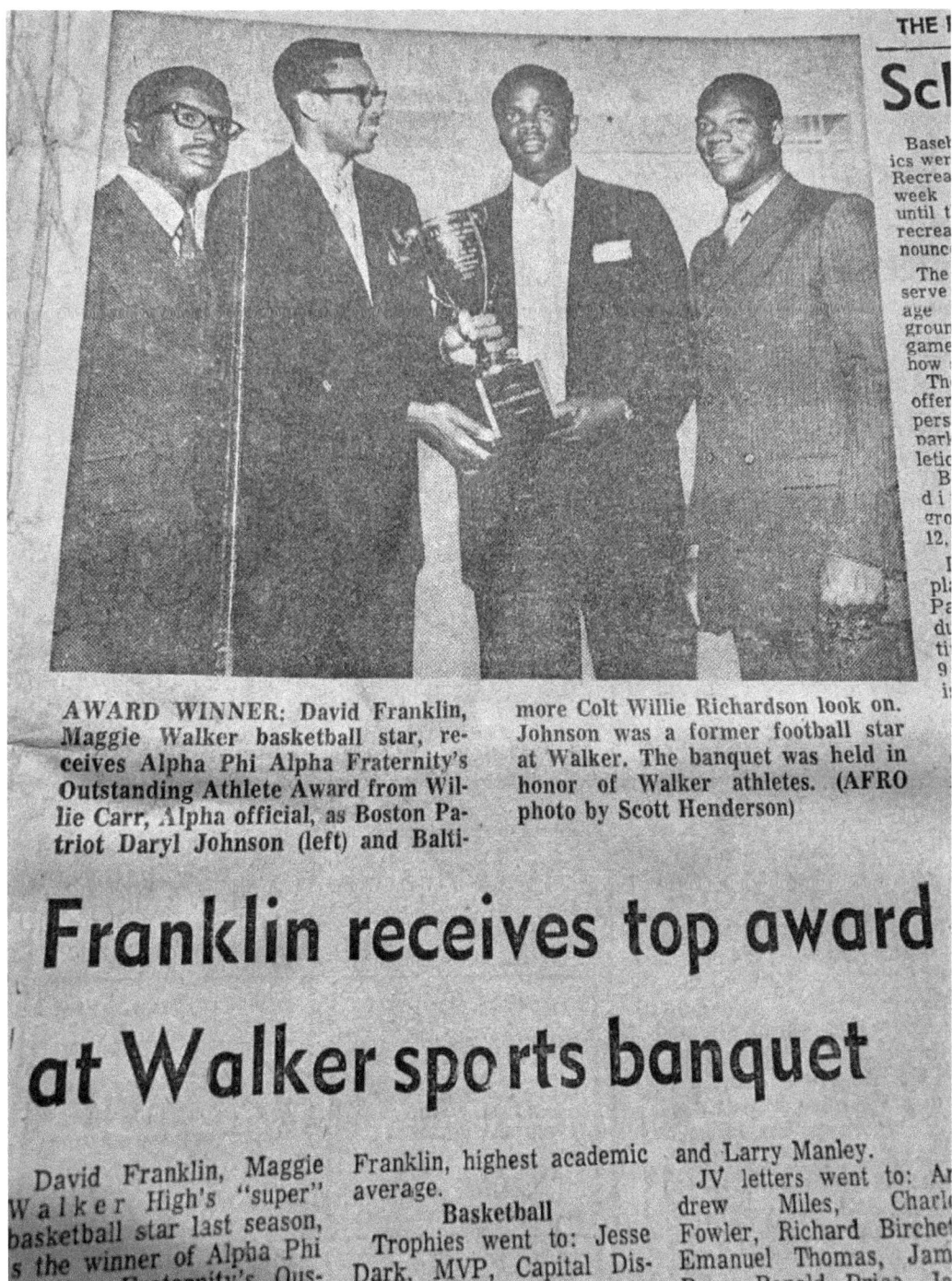

**Walker Sports Banquet Honors David Franklin
as Daryl Johnson and Willie Richardson Join the Celebration.**

OUR CHEERING SQUAD RESTS BEFORE GOING INTO "BATTLE." Alice Myers, Jean Conway, Grace Haskins, Beverly Alston, Patricia Leecost, Earlene Stewart, Vivian Flyth, Marian Loving, Joyce Bush, Martha Hinton, Marshae Johnson, Sandra Buchner, Beverly Robinson, Lillian Carter, Joyce Haley, Dianne Harris, and Simonetta Haley.

Maggie Walker
Cheerleaders

**Maggie Walker Majorettes and Band
Celebrating a Green Dragon Victory at City Stadium**

1945 MLW Football Team
We stand on the shoulders of those who came before us.

My mother, Evelyn Simms, pictured on right, was Miss Maggie L. Walker 1945.

My mother's graduation picture -1945

A Mother Introduces Her Son to Daryl Johnson

Sometimes I have to chuckle when my young athlete son tells me how HARD playing sports is today.

He says, "Mom — there's SO much competition out here that I MUST go to expensive sports camps AND have top of the line gear if I'm going to perform at the highest level!"

Really, Son??

Son, **let me introduce you to Daryl Johnson - a REAL athlete**.
His "gear" consisted of a neighborhood football and a few pairs of dungarees.

His "camps" were held daily in the segregated South, where he became proficient in "intercepting" bigotry and racism.
And his fiercest "competitor" was LIFE and figuring out how to "tackle" both personal and societal challenges.

So son, when you speak of how "hard" it is to be an athlete - do a little research on the *legends* of the sport and all THEY had to endure and overcome.

You'll find the only thing they needed to be great was the *WILL* and *WORK* to win… on and off the field.

LaJuan Carter-Dent and Son

College Years

2nd Quarter

You Play Football with Your Body and a Ball...

You Survive the Game with Skill and Brains

"The ideal attitude is to be physically loose and mentally tight" Arthur Ashe

HONOREES

DARYL JOHNSON — **FOOTBALL**

Daryl E. Johnson is a native of Richmond, Virginia and graduated from Maggie L. Walker High School. He entered Morgan State University in 1964 and received his Bachelor of Science in Business Administration degree. Mr. Johnson was a four year letterman in football playing on three undefeated Central Intercollegiate Athletic Association (CIAA) Championship Football teams from 1965-1967, and was a two-year letterman in track and field.

Mr. Johnson acquired many honors during his amazing football career; however, he carved his own piece of Morgan athletic history as the starting quarterback during the 1966 and 1967 CIAA Championship football seasons. In 1966, Morgan State University became the first predominantly African-American team selected to play in the Tangerine Bowl (now the Citrus Bowl). Mr. Johnson led the Morgan Bears on one of the biggest stages the University had been on to a historic 14-6 win over West Chester (Pa.) State. He ended the season being selected to the 1st Team Maryland All-State Team as a Place Kicker and 1st Team All-CIAA.

During the 1967 season, Mr. Johnson led the Bears to their third consecutive CIAA Championship and undefeated seasons. He set a school record by becoming the first quarterback to pass for over 1,000 yards in single season, completing 54 percent of his passes for 1,050 yards. His senior year performance was so outstanding that he was selected 1st Team Maryland All-State Team as quarterback, 1st Team All-CIAA Quarterback and 1st Team Pittsburg Courier Black All-American Defensive Back. Mr. Johnson also received the prestigious Pigskin Club of Washington D.C. Award for NCAA Small College Player of the Year. Mr. Johnson finished his career leading Morgan to the longest winning streak in college football at the time, 26 games. The Morgan football team only lost one game during Mr. Johnson's four year career.

Mr. Johnson was drafted in the eighth-round in 1968 by the Boston Patriots and played from 1968-1971, becoming a starter in his rookie season. He was selected to the Patriots' All-Star 1960-1969 Team by Patriots' fans. Mr. Johnson also played in the World Football League with the Houston Texans/Shreveport Steamer teams.

After his professional football career, Mr. Johnson achieved additional success in the corporate world as a stockbroker, small business owner and small business liaison. He currently resides in West Newbury, Massachusetts, where he is a self-employed sports consultant to professional, college and high school athletes and is a Master Mason of the Prince Hall Grand Lodge of Free & Accepted Masons of Massachusetts.

Morgan State said I carved my own piece of athletic history as a starting quarterback in 1966 and 1967.

In January 2016, Morgan's football players who played in the 1966 Tangerine Bowl were invited to return to Orlando and ride on the float. We were the first HBCU to be invited to play in the Tangerine Bowl. We were the champs. Today it is called Capital One/Buffalo Wings Bowl. I'm standing top left and Willie Lanier from Richmond, VA and Maggie L. Walker is seated center front.

Morgan Players Honored

**Team of Distinction Award, Morgan State Bears
1966 Tangerine Bowl Champs**

In 1964, when I was a freshman at Morgan, I was a wide receiver, catching passes from Gilbert Carter, also from Maggie L. Walker High School. I was team QB in 1966 and 1967.

Inspirational Sports Quotes

- "Don't give up at halftime; concentrate on winning the second half." – Paul Bear Bryant, former football player and coach
- "A winner never stops trying" Tom Landry, former Football player and coach
- "Success is not forever, and failure isn't fatal" – Don Shula, Former football cornerback and coach

My freshman year at Morgan, 1964

Inspirational Sports Quotes

- "Champions keep playing until they get it right. Sports build character, it teaches you to play by the rules, it teaches you to know what it feels like to win and lose—it teaches you about life." – Billy Jean King, Tennis champion
- "To succeed…you need to find something to hold on to, something to motivate you, something to inspire you." – Tony Dorsett, former NFL Running back
- When you have confidence, you can have a lot of fun. And when you have fun, you can do amazing things." – Joe Namath, former NFL quarterback
- "Nobody who ever gave his best regretted it" – George Halas, Former player and coach

**Athletic Hall of Fame, Grizzly Bear Award Presented by Varsity "M" Club
Morgan State University**

Morgan's Hall of Fame Salutes Daryl E. Johnson

Inspirational Sports Quotes

- "The game of life is a lot like football. You have to tackle your problems, block your fears, and score your points when you get the opportunity." – Lewis Gizzard, former American writer
- "When you win, you don't get carried away. But if you go step by step, with confidence, you can go far." – Diego Maradona – former player for Argentina, Barcelona, Napoli and later football coach
- "The principle is competing against yourself. It's about self-improvement, about being better than you were the day before." – Steve Young, former NFL Quarterback
- "Set your goals high, and don't stop till you get there." – Bo Jackson, former football player

THE MORGAN STATE UNIVERSITY INTERCOLLEGIATE ATHLETICS DEPARTMENT

Congratulates

The Varsity 'M' Club and its New Hall of Fame Inductees

Ronald Cloud, Swimming '71
Yvette Coleman, Track and Field '79
George Hubbard, Swimming '71
Paul Hubbard, Swimming '70
Daryl Johnson, Football '68
Kimberly Wood, Volleyball '95

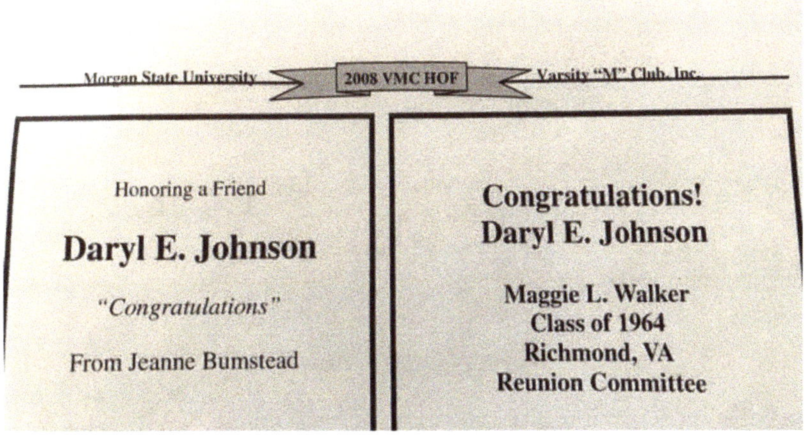

Morgan State University — 2008 VMC HOF — Varsity "M" Club, Inc.

Honoring a Friend

Daryl E. Johnson

"Congratulations"

From Jeanne Bumstead

Congratulations!
Daryl E. Johnson

Maggie L. Walker
Class of 1964
Richmond, VA
Reunion Committee

Daryl Johnson
NCAA Player of the Year 1967

presented by the Pigskin Club of Washington, DC

Football players had to take a dance class at Morgan. I danced to *Ave Maria*. The same muscle groups are used for *football and dancing*. My gracefulness is captured in this picture. Now you may laugh.

Friends gathered at the home of Nanette Kindle-Mitchell in 2008 to welcome Helen and me.
Back row, L-R: Friends, Eloise Foster, Glen, Gwendolyn Jones, Nanette, Helen, Michael's wife, Willie Montague, #12, my step uncle, James Simms, adopted by my grandparents when he was 10. Kneeling: the starting running backs for MLW #23 D. Johnson, #25 Fred Robinson, #25 Michael Johnson, Willie Montague also played in backfield.

I have found that friends we meet in school help teach us how to be patient and wait our turn. As we move into adulthood we learn more about taking responsibility, how to make a good first impression, how to become a conscious listener, how to read body language, how to apologize, how to set goals and how to protect your computer! Let's not forget how to sew on a button, how to apply the Heimlich Maneuver, how to grill vegetables and how to jump start your car*!*

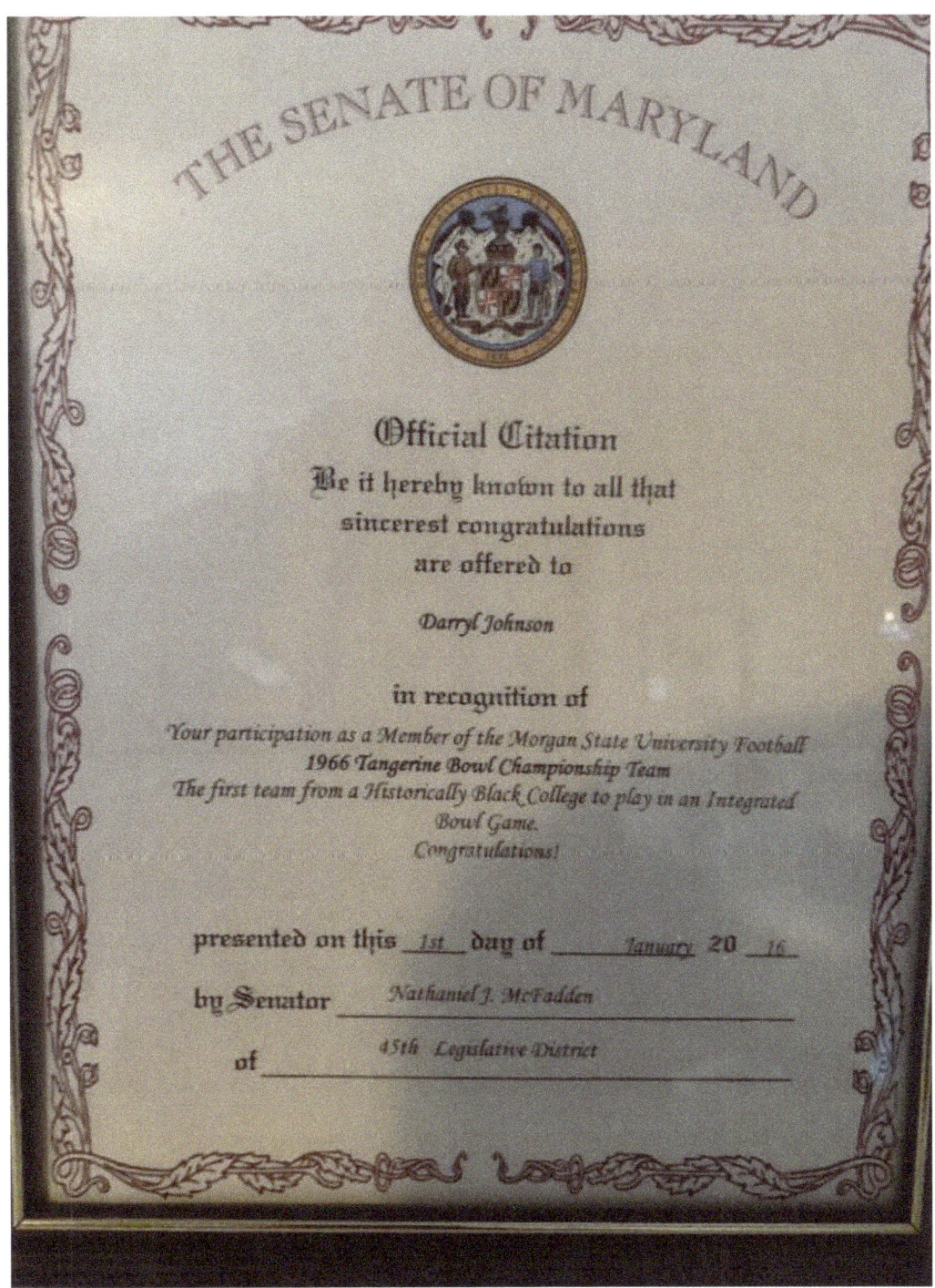

The Senate of Maryland thanks Morgan State Players for Tangerine Bowl Championship.

Johnson Paces Undefeated Bears

My best friend in college was Raymond Pollard. We spent time on the weekends discussing campus life and listening to music.

Notable alumni [edit]

Fifty two former Morgan players have gone on to play professional football. Thirty eight players went to the NFL, eight to the CFL, three to the WFL and one each to the AAFC, the Arena Football League and the AIFA. At least one player has gone to the NFL every decade since 1950 from Morgan State.[13]

Former Morgan Bears Len Ford, Leroy Kelly, Willie Lanier and Rosey Brown are members of the Pro Football Hall of Fame in Canton, Ohio.

Professional players

Player	Position	League	Team	Years	Ref
1940s					
Elmore Harris	RB	AAFC	Brooklyn Dodgers	1947	[14]
1950s					
Len Ford †	DE	NFL	Cleveland Browns	1950	
Charlie Robinson	G	NFL	Pittsburgh Steelers	1951	[15]
Rosey Brown †	OT	NFL	New York Giants	1952	[16]
1960s					
Oliver Dobbins	DB	NFL	Buffalo Bills	1964	[17]
Leroy Kelly †	RB	NFL	Cleveland Browns	1964	[18]
Willie Lanier †	LB	NFL	Kansas City Chiefs	1966	[19]
Tom Carr	DT	NFL	New Orleans Saints	1967	[20]
Carlton Dabney	DT	NFL	Atlanta Falcons	1968	[21]
Daryl Johnson	CB	NFL	Boston Patriots	1968	[22]
Alvin Mitchell	CB	NFL	Cleveland Browns	1968	[23]
Jeff Queen	LB	NFL	San Diego Chargers	1969	[24]
Clarence Scott	CB	NFL	Boston Patriots	1968	[25]
Bob Wade	CB	NFL	Pittsburgh Steelers	1969	[26]

Morgan State Game Scores

1964

53	Hampton	7
27	NC College	0
14	Maryland State	0
15	Howard	8
8	NC A&T	29
53	Virginia Union	0
6	Virginia State	13
36	Delaware State	6
40	Shaw	7
252		**70**

Won 7, Lost 2

1965

41	Hampton	0
33	NC College	0
33	Maryland State	21
31	NC A&T	6
7	Virginia Union	0
53	Virginia State	0
34	Delaware State	0
33	Norfolk State	0
265		**27**
36	Florida A&M	7

**Orange Blossom Classic
(Miami, FL)**

Won 9, Lost 0

1966

69	Hampton	0
21	NC College	0
12	Maryland State	8
13	NC A&T	8
66	Virginia Union	7
65	Virginia State	0
38	Delaware State	0
284		**23**
14	West Chester St.	**6**

NCAA Atlantic Coast Championship
Tangerine Bowl
National Champions

NCAA Atlantic Coast Championship
Tangerine Bowl
National Champions

Won 8, Lost 0

1967

28	Hampton	13
23	NC College	0
36	Maryland State	26
27	NC A&T	20
47	Virginia Union	16
34	Virginia State	3
27	Delaware State	0
63	Norfolk State	0
285		**78**

Won 8, Lost 0

Professional Football

3rd Quarter

Patriots Sign Daryl Johnson

BOSTON — (UPI) — The Boston Patriots have signed their eighth-round draft choice, quarterback Daryl Johnson of Morgan State College (Md.)

Johnson, a 5-foot-11, 190-pounder who has been clocked in an exceptional 4.4 seconds for 40 yards, will be tried as a safety at first, the patriots said.

A native of Richmond, Va., who now lives in Baltimore, Johnson led Morgan State to what is currently the longest winning streak in college football—26 games—with a 54.3 per cent completion record and 19 touchdown passes as a junior and senior.

Rommie Loudd, director of player personnel for the Patriots, said, "we considered him our No. 1 sleeper prospect in the country as far as potential was concerned and this was before we knew we were going to get him."

Daryl Johnson Signed by the Boston Patriots

The BOSTON PATRIOTS — Champions Eastern Division 1963
FOOTBALL CLUB

FENWAY PARK
BOSTON, MASS. 02215
Tel. 262-6363

WILLIAM H. SULLIVAN JR.
President

CLIVE H. RUSH
Head Coach

October 17, 1969

Daryl Johnson
112 Middle Street
Weymouth, Mass.

Dear Daryl:

You will be happy to know that your picture will be on the chewing gum cards next year. For that reason, we have to set up a frantic picture taking session Sunday during the pre-game warm-up. The photographer understands that you will not have any spare time so he is prepared to take the pictures quickly. (I am sending this note to each of the 17 players involved).

Sincerely,

Eileen Maney

Eileen Maney
Public Relations

E
M
/
b
e
p

BUFFALO BILLS • HOUSTON OILERS   DENVER BRONCOS • KANSAS CITY CHIEFS
MIAMI DOLPHINS • NEW YORK JETS   SAN DIEGO CHARGERS • OAKLAND RAIDERS
• BOSTON PATRIOTS •   • CINCINNATI BENGALS •

My picture made it on the Boston Patriots Chewing Gum Card — what's your flavor?

The Topps Vault Authenticated Professional Memorabilia

Inspirational Sports Quotes

- "It doesn't matter where you come from, what you have or don't have…all you need to have is faith in God, an undying passion for what you do and what you choose to do in this life, and a relentless drive and the will to do whatever it takes to be successful in whatever you put your mind to." – Stephen Curry, NBA Champion
- "In life, you won't go far unless you know where to locate the goalpost" – Paul Brown, former coach
- "The difference between a successful person and others is not a lack of strength, not a lack of knowledge, but rather a lack of Will" – Vince Lombardy, former football coach
- "Aim for the sky and you'll reach the ceiling. Aim for the ceiling and you'll stay on the floor" – Bill Shankly, Scottish Football manager

My daughter framed this jersey.

Back in the late sixties, the NFL only allowed black shoes, except for Joe Namath. He was allowed to wear white. I died my shoes red and tried to wear them in a game. Pete Rozelle, the commissioner at the time, would not allow my red shoes. Look at the colors the kids are wearing today in the NFL! They called my dyed red shoes "out of uniform." I think I did a great job dying my black shoes red!

The Starting Defensive Backfield of the 1970 Boston/New England Patriots.

(L to R) Daryl Johnson #23, 26 Clarence Scott, 42 Don Webb, 41 Larry Carwell, Bill Elias, DB coach, and Cleve Rush, Head Coach

Daryl Johnson (23) on the move after intercepting a Namath pass. Running inteference is Schottenheimer (54). (Photo by Robert Houston)

1969 - I intercepted a Joe Namath pass—*that was a big deal back in the day to intercept a pass from Broadway Joe.*

Frustrated by missing a pass in a game against San Diego…so what did I do? I tried to leave the planet by jumping high as I could, but gravity pulled my behind back to Earth. We lost 13-10.

I'm tackling O.J Simpson here. In football you must be fearless, I guess I was crazy too.

Watch Your Temper

The Mayo Clinic reports that anger is a normal and even healthy emotion but it's important to deal with it in a positive way. Uncontrolled anger can take a toll on both your health and your relationships.

Buffalo Bills Hurdle Over Daryl Johnson, #23

Hit Em Hard

O.J. On the Move!

Always Looking for the Ball

Number 15 is Jack Kemp. President Obama awarded him the *Presidential Medal of Freedom* in 2009.

Daryl led Morgan State's football team to two undefeated seasons, and then he played in the pros for the Patriots. He states in this article, "it was a life you dream about as a kid… then while you are living it, you can't believe it."

*Check out Top Right
of this Cartoon*

"Daryl Johnson grabbed Hoyle Granger's fumble and scooted 32 yards for a Pats' TD!"
When I saw I was in a cartoon, it was so very funny to me.
A good laugh is wonderful.

Laughter

Steve Wilson, a psychologist, says if people can get more laughter in their lives, they will be much better off. It strengthens your immune system, boosts mood and diminishes pain and protects you from the damaging effects of stress.

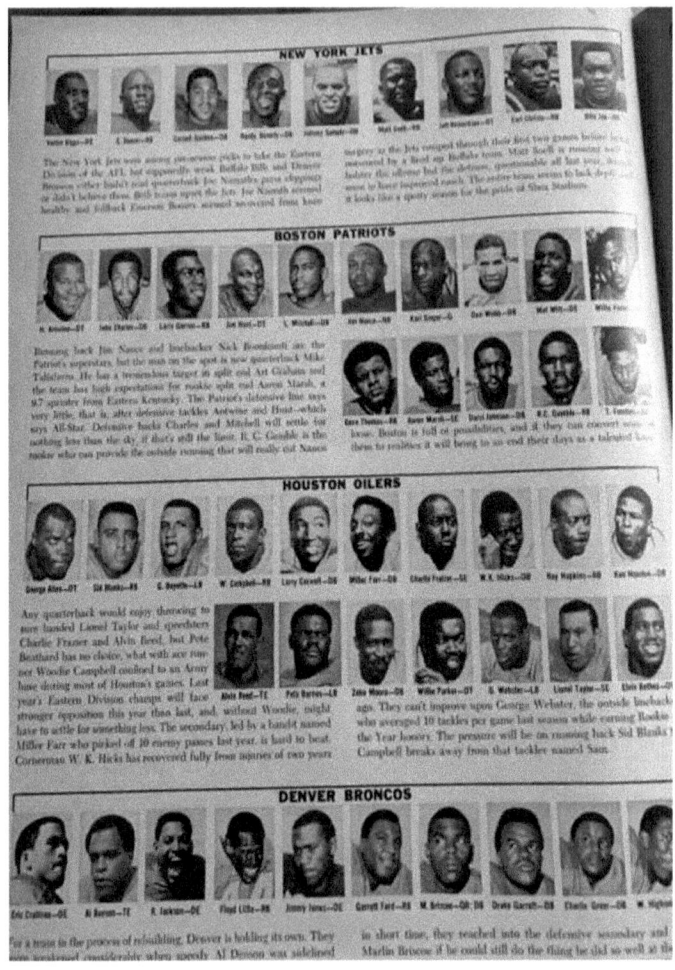

Ebony Magazine celebrated all Black professional football players. I'm above with Patriots.

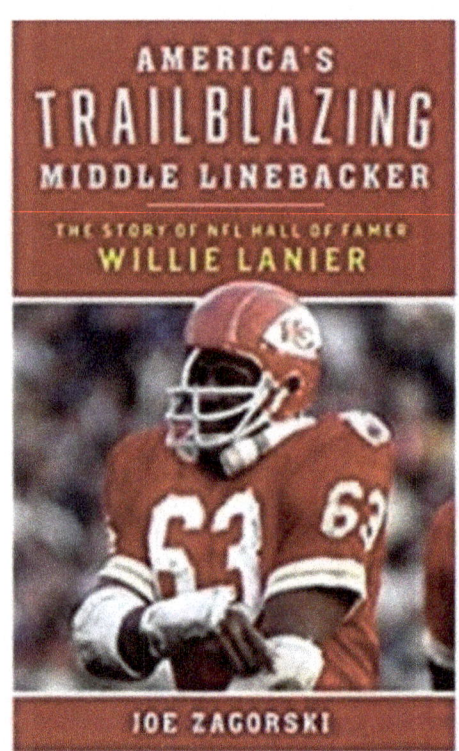

AMAZON.COM

America's Trailblazing Middle Linebacker: The Sto...

Willie Lanier was the first African-American middle linebacker in pro football history, playing for the Kansas City Chiefs from 1967-1977 in an era when d...

Cheers for Maggie Walker's Willie Lanier
First African American middle linebacker in Pro football history.
We played together at Maggie L. Walker and Morgan.

Patriots playing cards with my picture, a gift from daughter Brandi.

Life After the Patriots

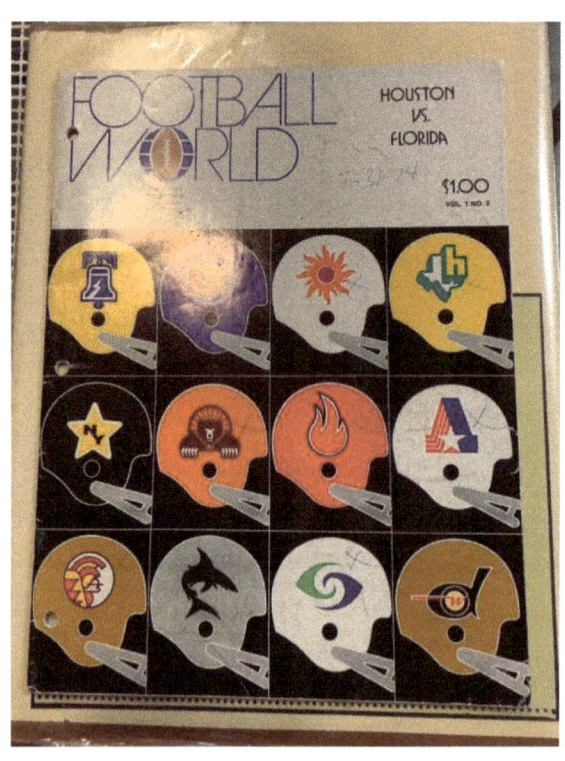

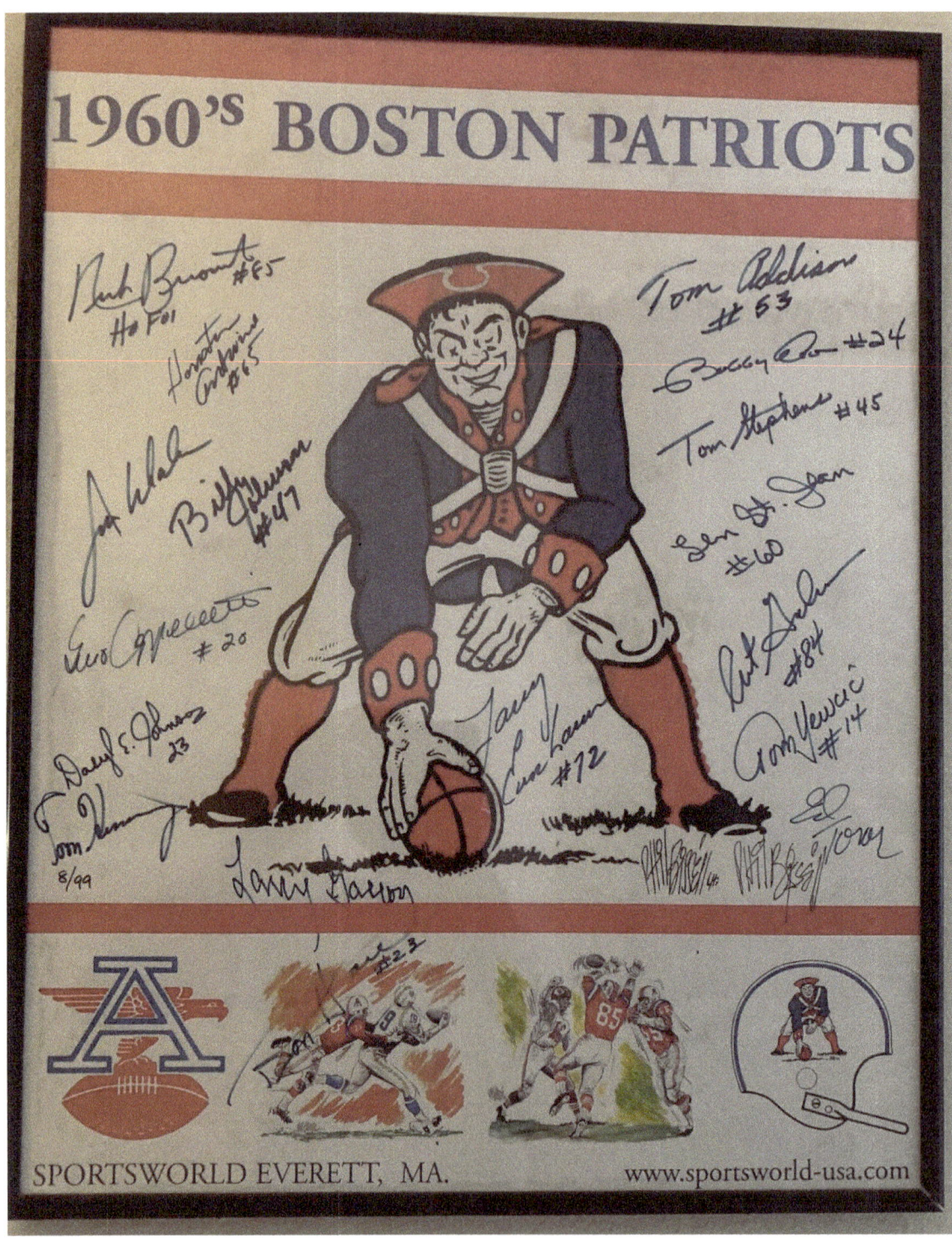

As of August 2020, there are only six players alive who signed this.

When you are a professional player,
your photo may appear anywhere. This is a can! (*right photo bottom*).

Family

4th Quarter

This is Helen, my wife of 34 years, she has the biggest heart. I finally got it right. She says I'm funny and I say she is kind, gracious, encouraging and beautiful, inside and out.

Daryl and Daughter Brandi

What I wanted most for my daughter, she has accomplished — a professional career as she embraces motherhood with confidence. Brandi is my heart.

My Son, Deron Johnson, also loves football. He outgrew my lap but never my heart.

Daughter, Brandi, and my granddaughter, Nevaeh

Granddaughter Nevaeh
Nevaeh and I play Putt-Putt September 2019

Because grandpa came out to play, Nevaeh says she allowed me to win!

Brandi's Daughter, Nevaeh

Nevaeh says, VOTE!

Relaxing at Home　　　　Son, Deron

Baby Brandi   **Baby Nevaeh**

Helen and Granddaughter Nevaeh

A Family Moment

Evelyn Simms Johnson-Blair
My Mother, My Rock, my Guiding Light

Mom would challenge me with something difficult that tested the strength of my nerves, my aptitude, my attitude, and wisdom to do things diligently and differently. She obviously gave me my sense of style.

My Mother Evelyn Simms Johnson-Blair

My Grandfather, Deacon Sidney Simms

My Maternal Grandparents, Sidney and Leila Simms,

Nanny and Honey

Missy and Molly
Beloved Family Felines

My grandfather built this house in Chesterfield, VA.
I was born here and have many fond memories.

My Hobby is Latch Hook Art

Strong as a Lion and Gentle as a Lamb
It took me 4 months to complete this piece of art

**Strength is the Ability to do Things that Require
a Lot of Physical and or Mental Effort**

It's the choice to continue through the pain even when it feels unbearably hard. The gentle person attracts the trust of others. Gentleness is a strong hand with a soft touch. It is a tender, compassionate approach towards others' weaknesses and limitations. A gentle person still speaks the truth, even painful truth but in a way it's well received.

White Tiger

The white tiger is a
pigmentation variance
of the Bengal tiger.
The human race has numerous
beautiful *pigmentation variances*.

Skating Snoopy

Snoopy is 600 square inches (30x20). I latched this in 2017, and *it took me a couple of months*. There were 9 to 10 different yarn colors. The mat was blank. There are mats with the color design imprinted on them. The more yarn colors, the more difficult especially if it's a blank mat. Peanut characters have always been my favorite.

A Place of Solitude

Two and a half months to complete the church.
Discover inner peace and love through mindfulness.
Live a life of fellowship, learn to increase love.

2020 Artwork

The Birth of Christ

Six months to create this latch hook. I believe all adults should learn how to create something beautiful with their hands. It is good mental therapy.

Three Owls

I donated this latch hook to my dialysis center.

2020 Artwork

In ancient times cats were worshiped as gods; they have never forgotten this!

Baby Green Dragon

2020 Artwork

Nature's great masterpiece. The only harmless huge thing.

"Cats are connoisseurs of comfort." – James Herriot

L to R
O.J. Anderson, NY Giants RB and MVP of Super Bowl, my wife Helen, me and daughter, Brandi.

"Please, no cameras— I'm relaxing."

Brother Ronnie and me

Like sands through the hourglass… so are the days of our lives.
Brother Ronnie

Something about this car I really liked.

*Giving Back
Paying Forward*

Overtime

This picture was in the Belmont Newspaper. I'm in the doorway of a clothing store I co-owned in Belmont, MA. My partner was Jewish, and our store was across the street from the John Birch Society. I guess I was considered provocative in those days, *without* marching.

Becoming a Mason broadened my life. It's like an exclusive club that is faith and community service based. It's a lot of work, but the friendships you make are life-long.

I became a Mason at the age of 41

Employment

I have held a number of varied jobs while in college and after my football years. Working in different arenas contributed to my growth and gave me the confidence and tools to be a guest speaker to all types of audiences.

Here are some of my jobs:

Probation Officer, Stoughton District Court
Stockbroker, Bache-Halsey, Stewart, Shields, Model, Roland, Inc. Insurance
Adjuster for Kemper Insurance
A General Contractor
Radio Host, my own talk radio sports show Chrysler
Avco / Textron
New England Patriots
Saugus High School Track Coach

Guest Speaker
When speaking to audiences I would always give a short course in *Human Relations*. Coach Banks taught us the following and said we should remember throughout life:
6 Most Important Words: *I admit I made a mistake.*
5 Most Important Words: *You did a good job.*
4 Most Important Words: *What is your opinion?*
3 Most Important Words: *If you please.*
2 Most Important Words: *Thank You!*
1 Most Important Word: *WE.*

I quit working for Chrysler Corporation and joined the World Football League in Houston, TX. We were called the Houston Texans. The league folded in two years. It's quite a job to play football— that's the jackass in me. Maybe I can blame it on all the concussions I had, but it was my life, and I loved it.

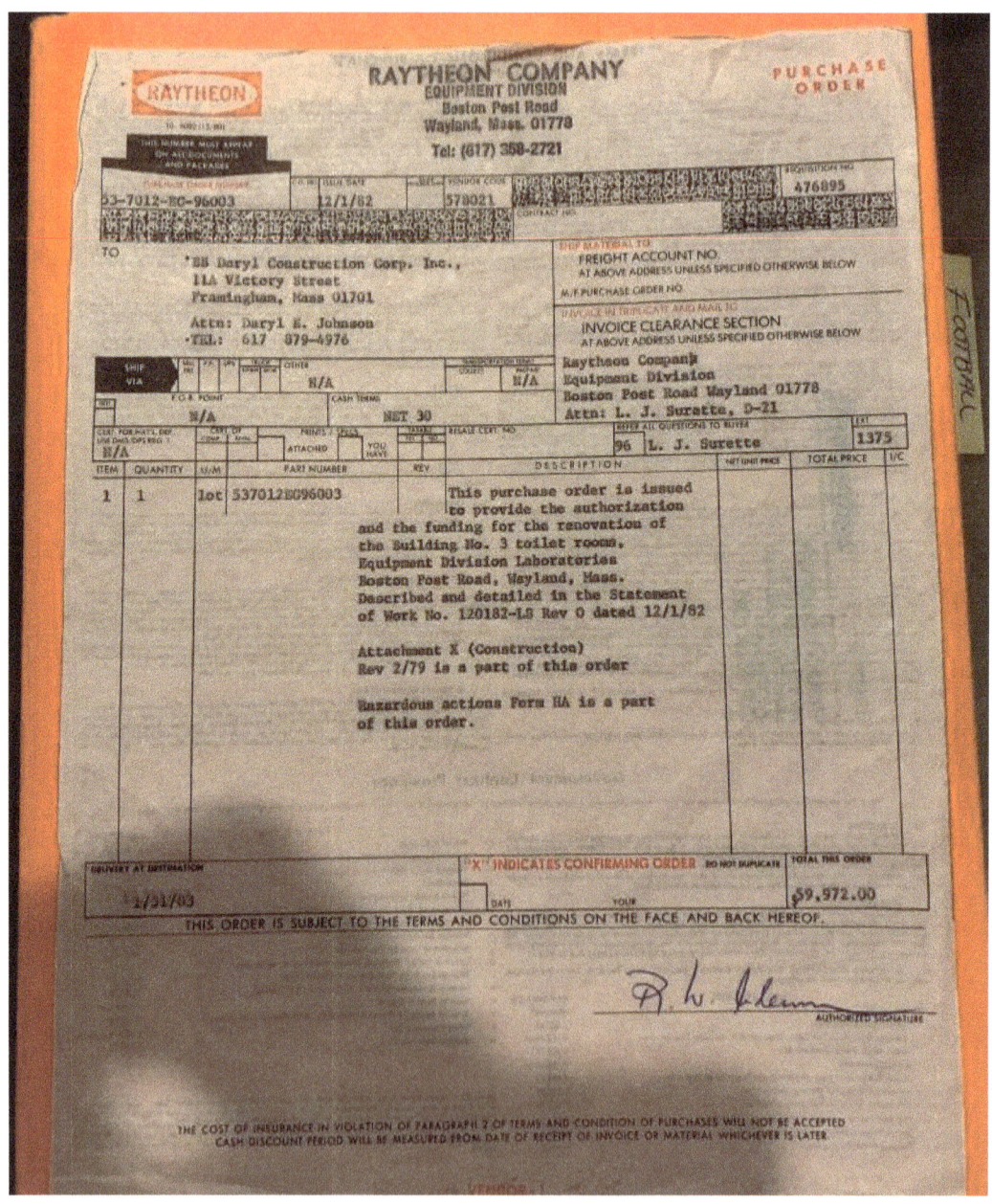

The construction business was rough! Controlled by the Mafia, I soon realized it was not for me. I wanted my talents elsewhere.

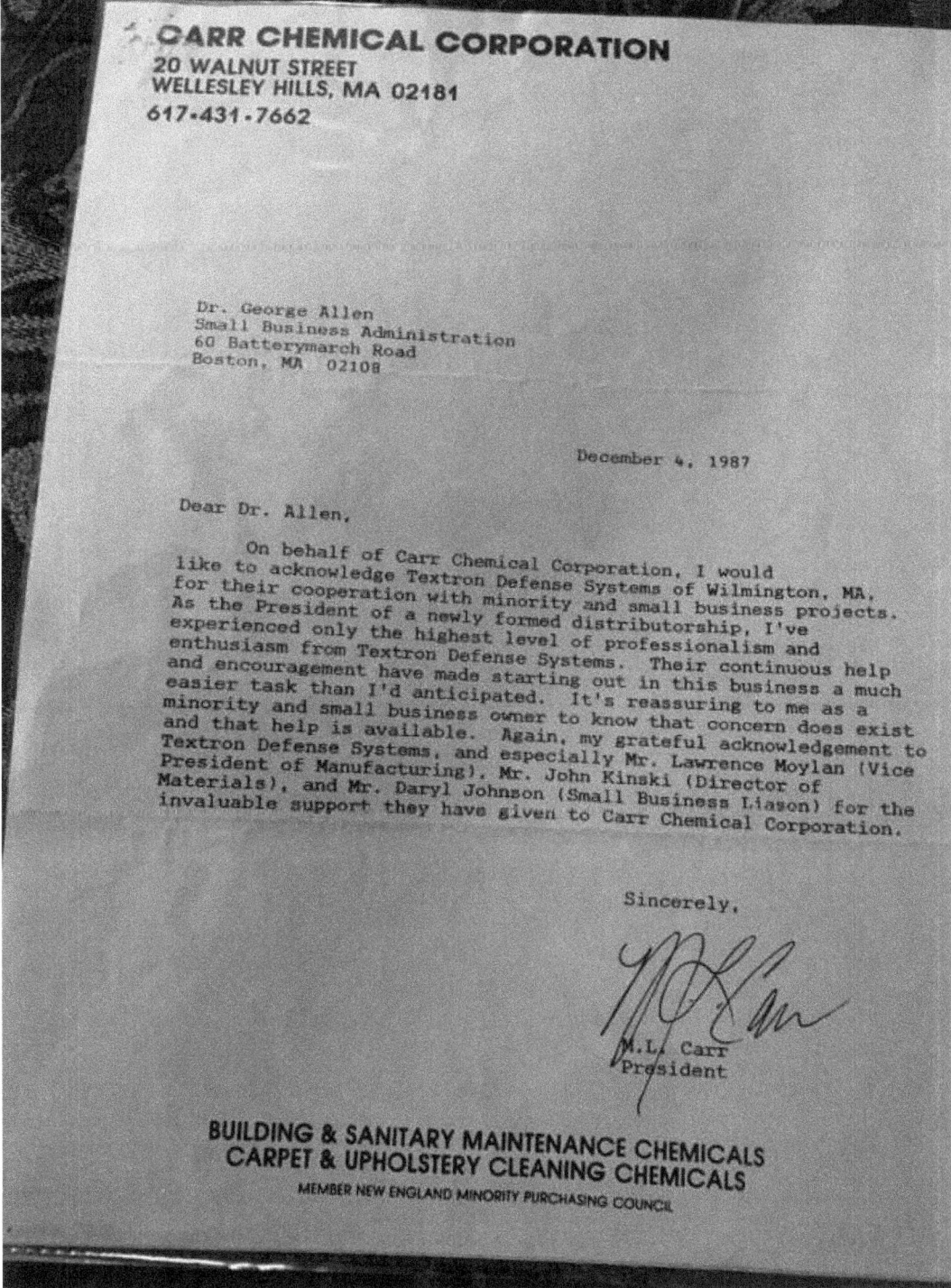

Letter from the President of Carr Chemical Corporation

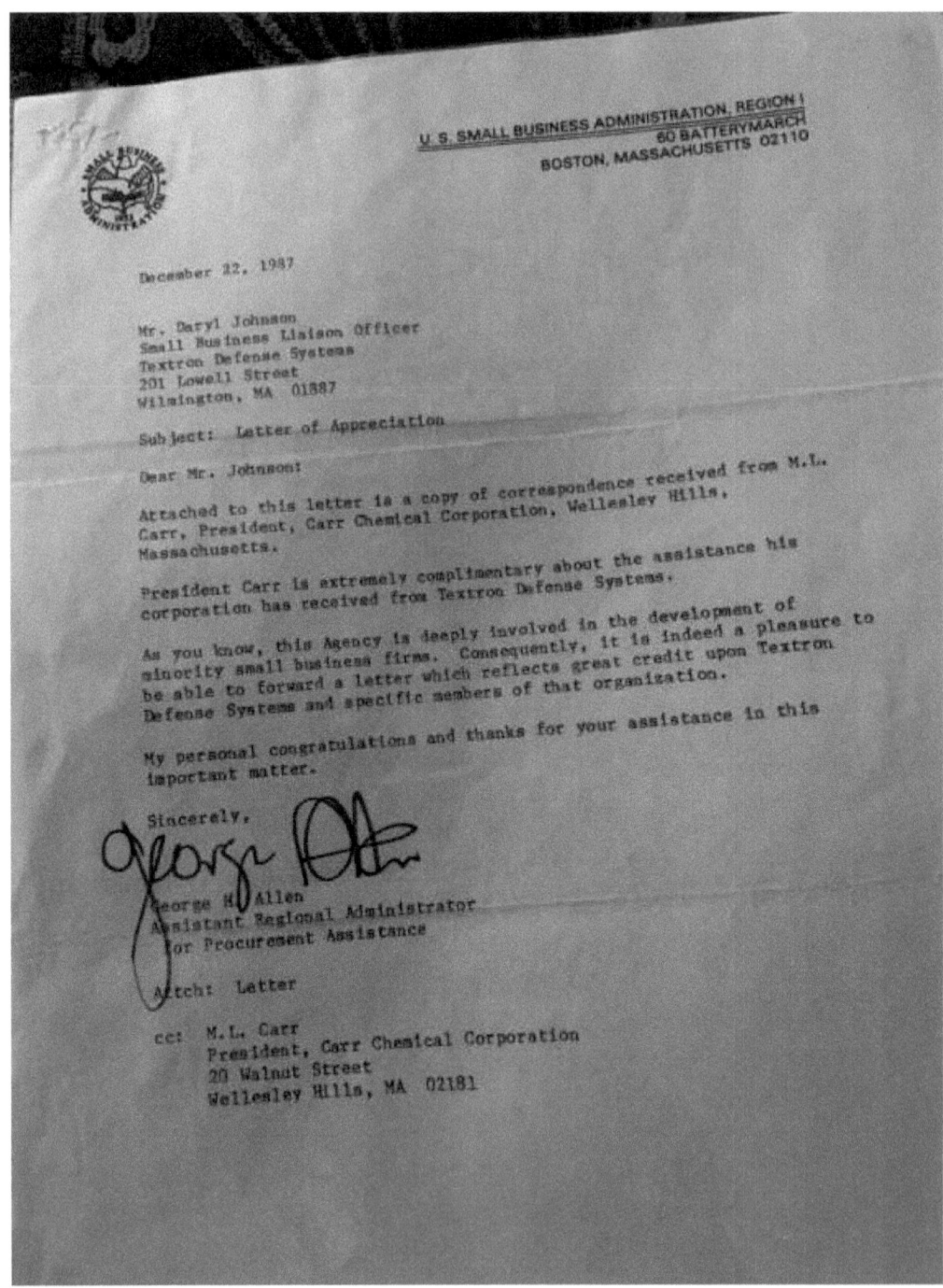

The Small Business Administration in Boston passes along a letter of appreciation to me from the President of Carr Chemical for Textron's assistance in a minority and small business project.

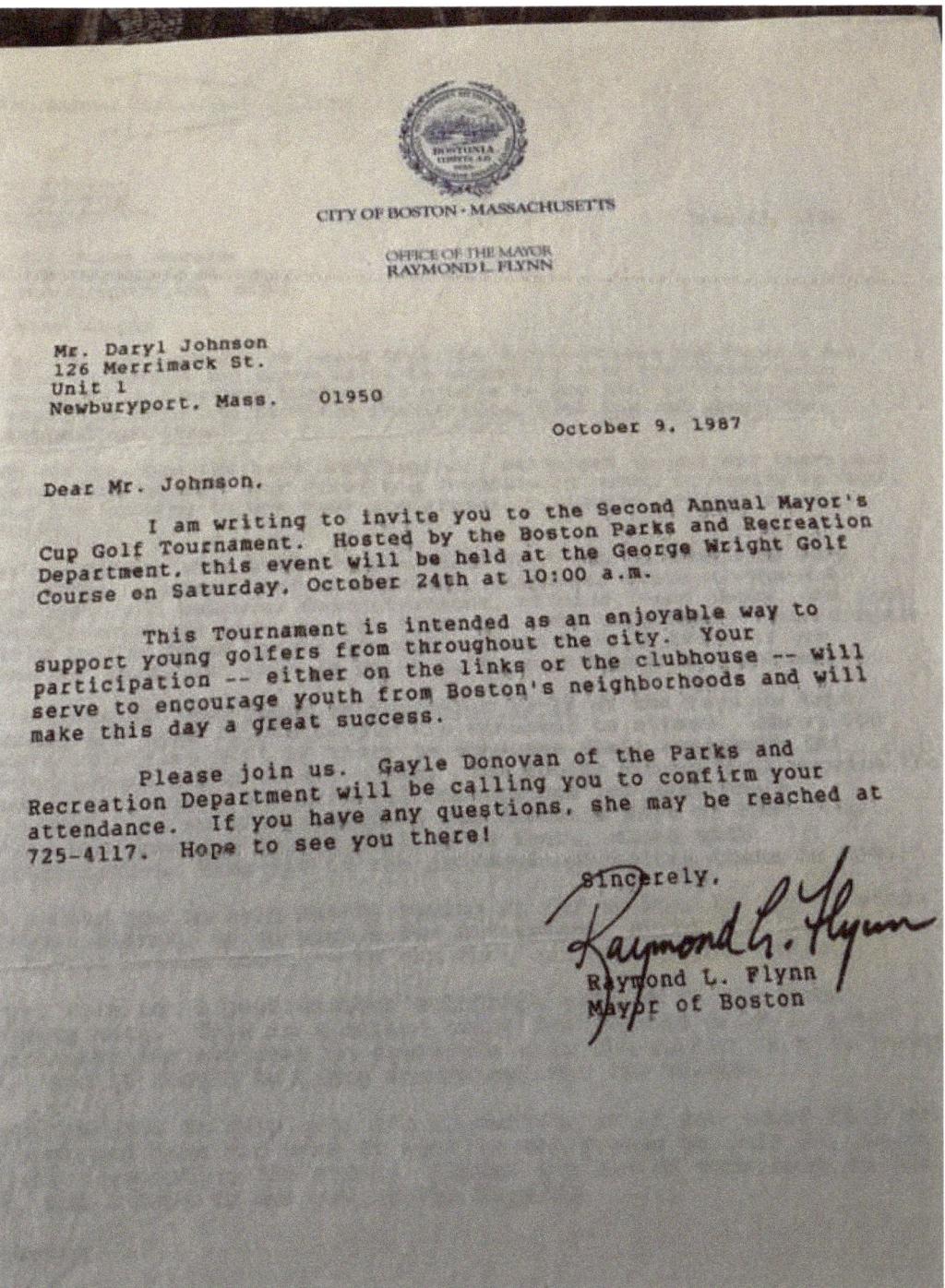

The City of Boston invited me to play in
The Annual Mayor's Cup Golf Tournament.

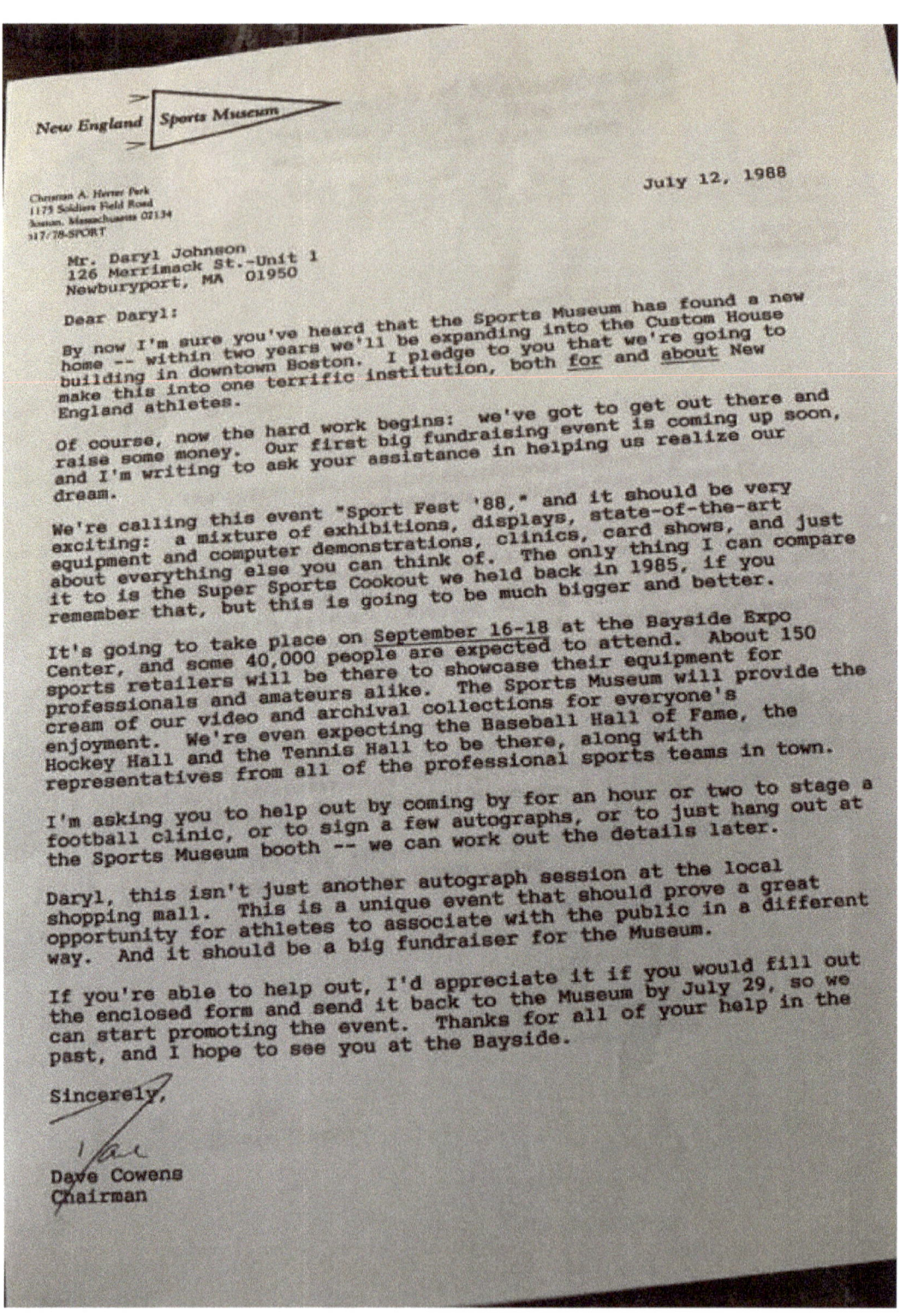

New England Sports Museum invited me to conduct a football clinic and sign autographs at a benefit and fundraiser for the museum.

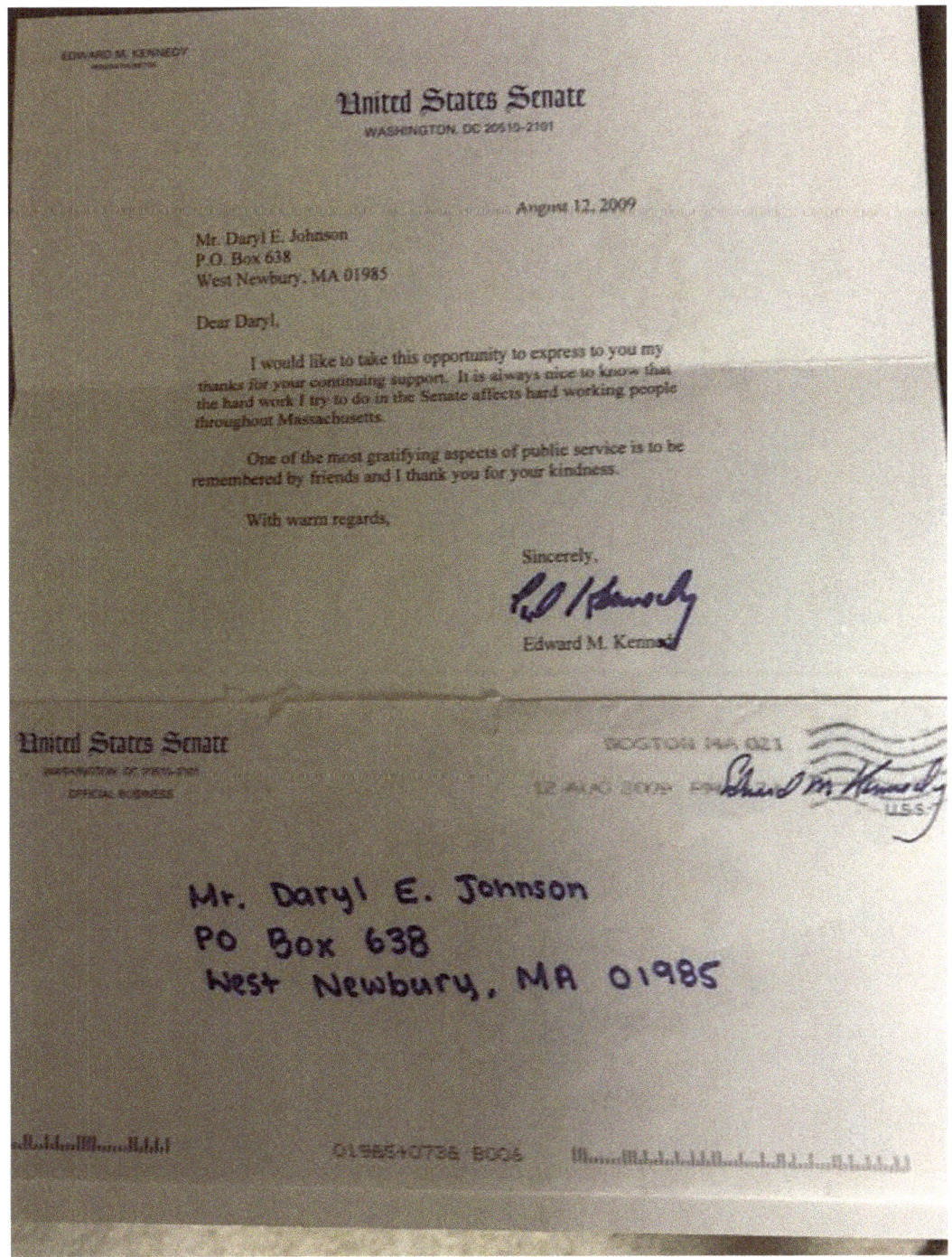

A personal note from Senator Edward M. Kennedy.

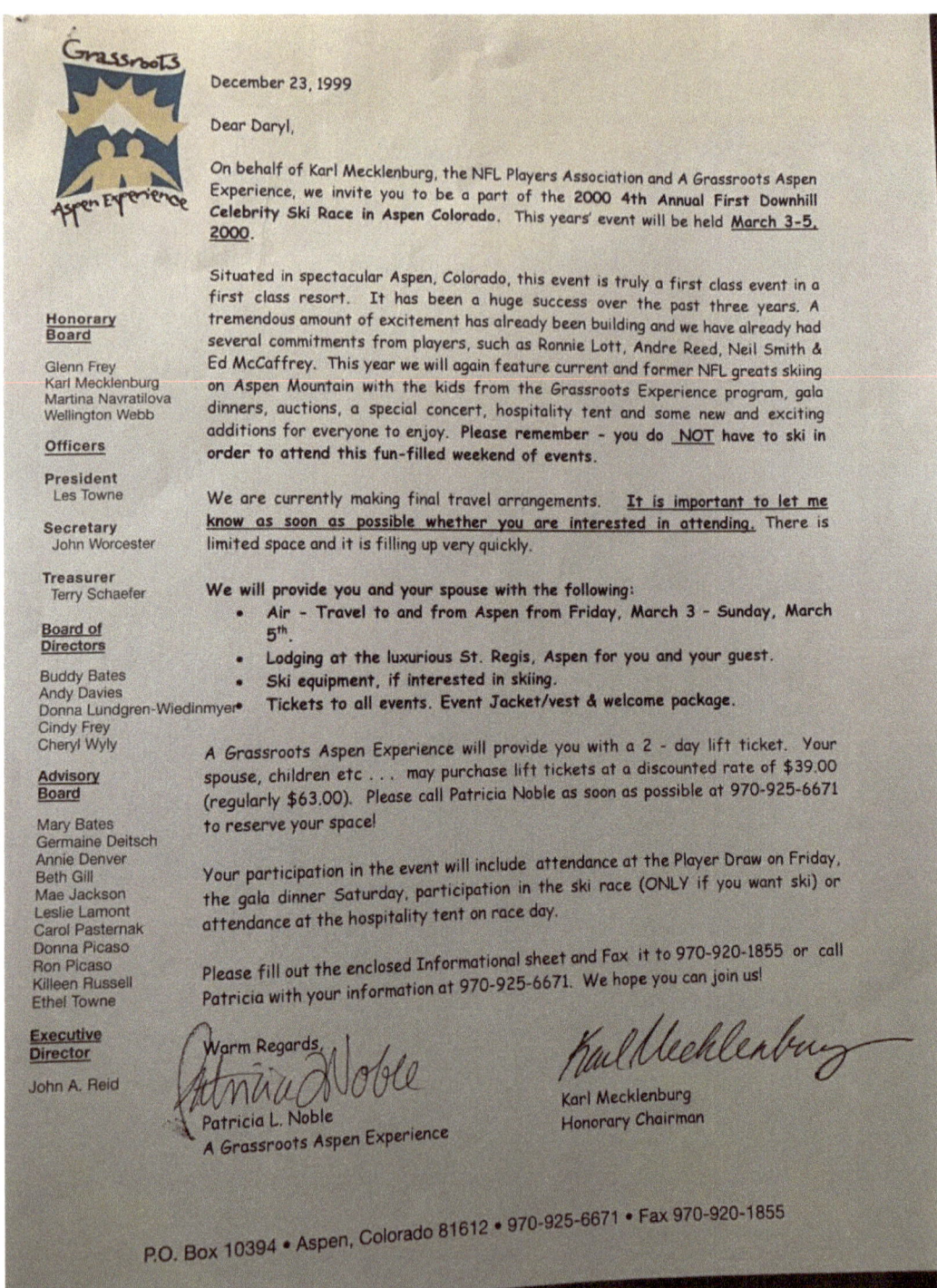

An invitation to participate in the first Downhill Celebrity Ski Race in Aspen, Colorado

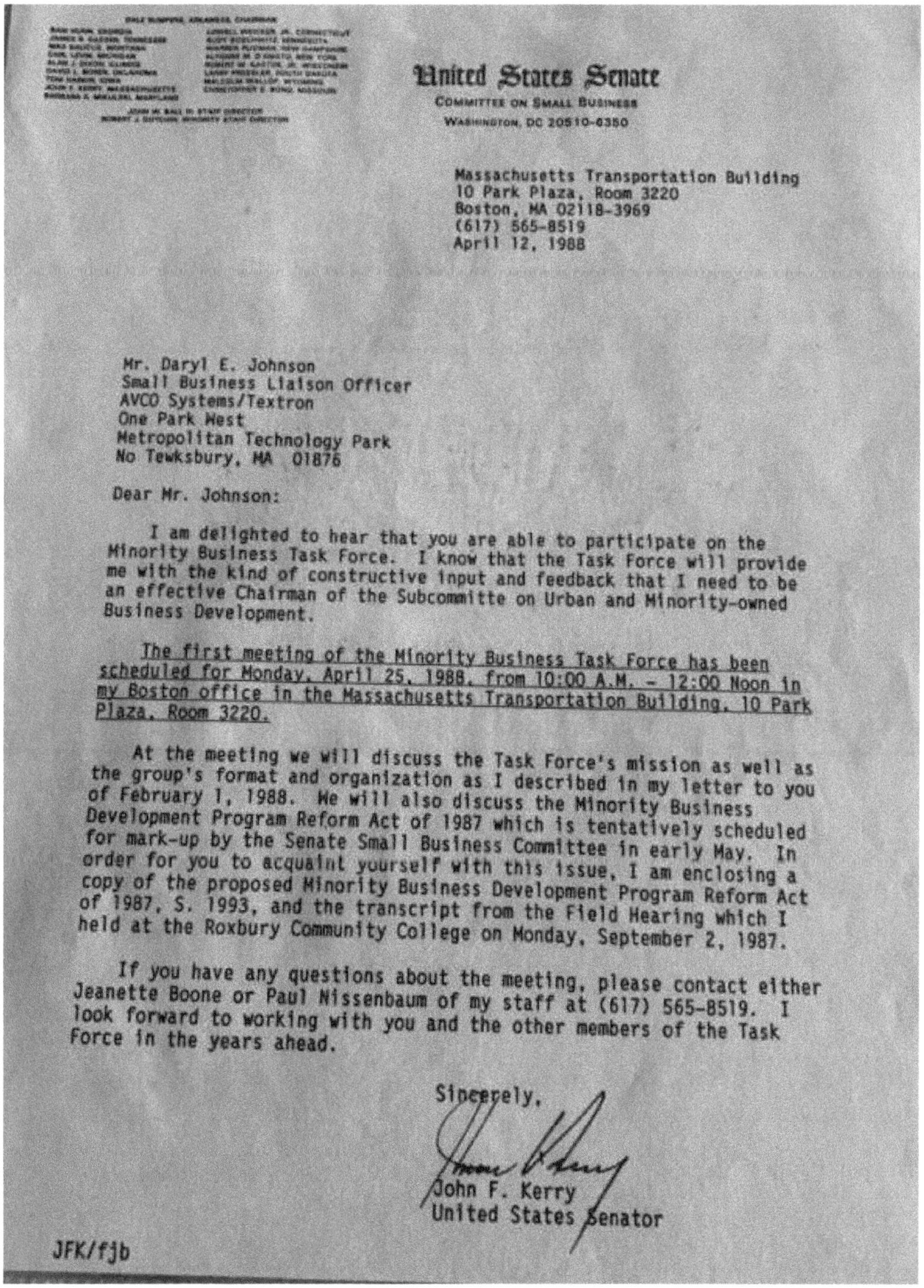

United States Senate
COMMITTEE ON SMALL BUSINESS
WASHINGTON, DC 20510-6350

Massachusetts Transportation Building
10 Park Plaza, Room 3220
Boston, MA 02118-3969
(617) 565-8519
April 12, 1988

Mr. Daryl E. Johnson
Small Business Liaison Officer
AVCO Systems/Textron
One Park West
Metropolitan Technology Park
No Tewksbury, MA 01876

Dear Mr. Johnson:

I am delighted to hear that you are able to participate on the Minority Business Task Force. I know that the Task Force will provide me with the kind of constructive input and feedback that I need to be an effective Chairman of the Subcommitte on Urban and Minority-owned Business Development.

<u>The first meeting of the Minority Business Task Force has been scheduled for Monday, April 25, 1988, from 10:00 A.M. - 12:00 Noon in my Boston office in the Massachusetts Transportation Building, 10 Park Plaza, Room 3220.</u>

At the meeting we will discuss the Task Force's mission as well as the group's format and organization as I described in my letter to you of February 1, 1988. We will also discuss the Minority Business Development Program Reform Act of 1987 which is tentatively scheduled for mark-up by the Senate Small Business Committee in early May. In order for you to acquaint yourself with this issue, I am enclosing a copy of the proposed Minority Business Development Program Reform Act of 1987, S. 1993, and the transcript from the Field Hearing which I held at the Roxbury Community College on Monday, September 2, 1987.

If you have any questions about the meeting, please contact either Jeanette Boone or Paul Nissenbaum of my staff at (617) 565-8519. I look forward to working with you and the other members of the Task Force in the years ahead.

Sincerely,

John F. Kerry
United States Senator

JFK/fjb

John Kerry thanked me for participating on the Minority Business Task Force

A guest speaker at Hartford High School in 1971 and sharing my journey gave me more reasons to count my blessings.

Inspirational Sports Quotes

- "Without self-discipline, success is impossible, period." – Lou Holtz, football coach and sportscaster
- "Your talent determines what you can do. Your motivation determines how much you are willing to do. Your attitude determines how well you do it." – Lou Holtz, former football coach
- "Life is ten percent what happens to you and ninety percent how you respond to it. – Lou Holtz
- "Confidence doesn't come out of nowhere. It's a result of something…hours and days and weeks and years of constant work and dedication." – Robert Staubach, former NFL quarterback

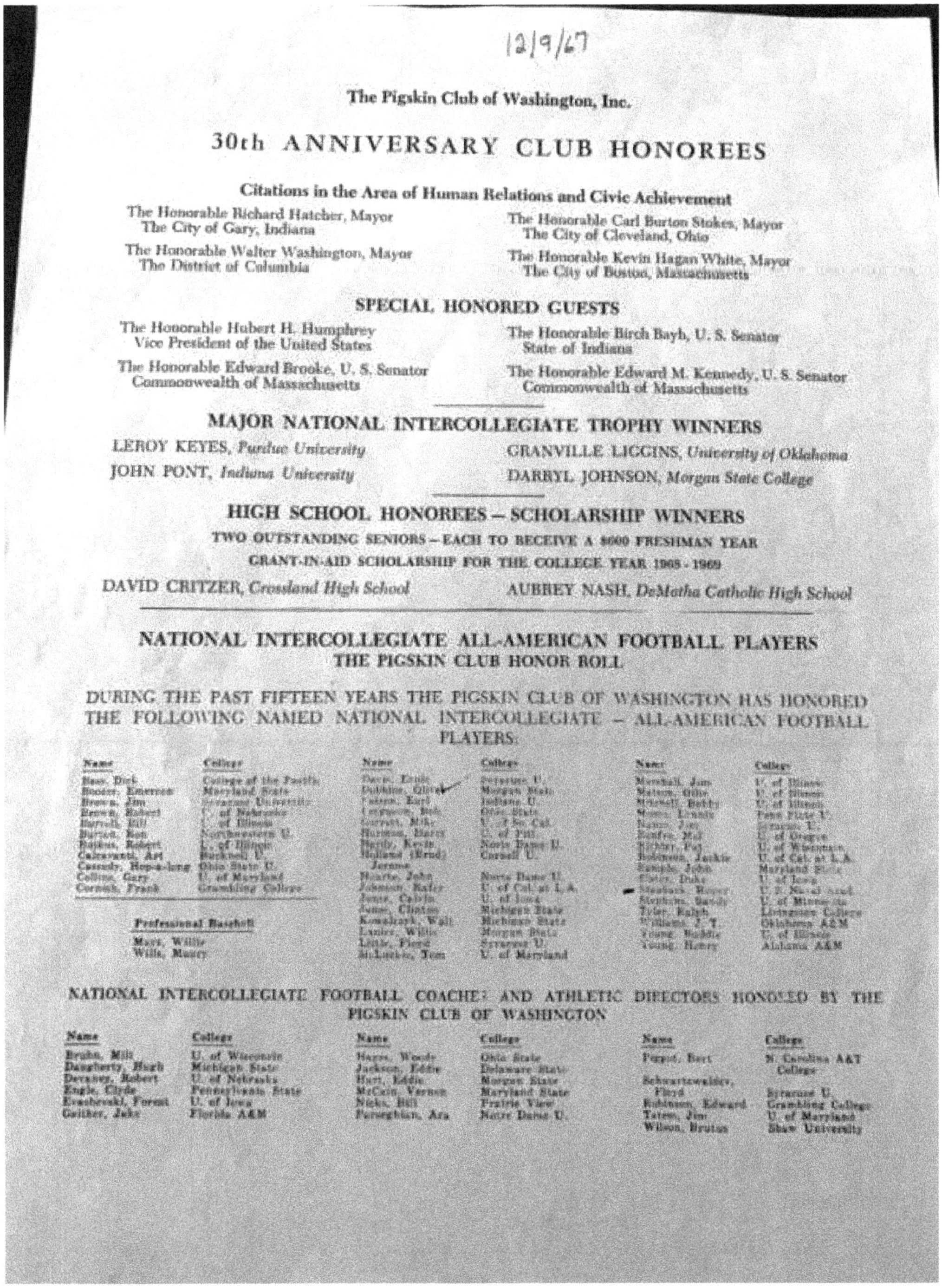

12/9/67

The Pigskin Club of Washington, Inc.

30th ANNIVERSARY CLUB HONOREES

Citations in the Area of Human Relations and Civic Achievement

The Honorable Richard Hatcher, Mayor
The City of Gary, Indiana

The Honorable Walter Washington, Mayor
The District of Columbia

The Honorable Carl Burton Stokes, Mayor
The City of Cleveland, Ohio

The Honorable Kevin Hagan White, Mayor
The City of Boston, Massachusetts

SPECIAL HONORED GUESTS

The Honorable Hubert H. Humphrey
Vice President of the United States

The Honorable Edward Brooke, U. S. Senator
Commonwealth of Massachusetts

The Honorable Birch Bayh, U. S. Senator
State of Indiana

The Honorable Edward M. Kennedy, U. S. Senator
Commonwealth of Massachusetts

MAJOR NATIONAL INTERCOLLEGIATE TROPHY WINNERS

LEROY KEYES, *Purdue University*
JOHN PONT, *Indiana University*
GRANVILLE LIGGINS, *University of Oklahoma*
DARRYL JOHNSON, *Morgan State College*

HIGH SCHOOL HONOREES – SCHOLARSHIP WINNERS

TWO OUTSTANDING SENIORS – EACH TO RECEIVE A $600 FRESHMAN YEAR GRANT-IN-AID SCHOLARSHIP FOR THE COLLEGE YEAR 1968 - 1969

DAVID CRITZER, *Crossland High School*
AUBREY NASH, *DeMatha Catholic High School*

NATIONAL INTERCOLLEGIATE ALL-AMERICAN FOOTBALL PLAYERS
THE PIGSKIN CLUB HONOR ROLL

DURING THE PAST FIFTEEN YEARS THE PIGSKIN CLUB OF WASHINGTON HAS HONORED THE FOLLOWING NAMED NATIONAL INTERCOLLEGIATE – ALL-AMERICAN FOOTBALL PLAYERS:

Name	College	Name	College	Name	College
Bass, Dick	College of the Pacific	Davis, Ernie	Syracuse U.	Marshall, Jim	U. of Illinois
Bowser, Emerson	Maryland State	Dobbins, Oliver	Morgan State	Matson, Ollie	U. of Illinois
Brown, Jim	Syracuse University	Faison, Earl	Indiana U.	Mitchell, Bobby	U. of Illinois
Brown, Robert	U. of Nebraska	Ferguson, Bob	Ohio State	Moore, Lenny	Penn State U.
Burrell, Bill	U. of Illinois	Garrett, Mike	U. of So. Cal.	Nance, Jim	Syracuse U.
Burton, Ron	Northwestern U.	Harmon, Harry	U. of Pitt	Renfro, Mel	U. of Oregon
Butkus, Robert	U. of Illinois	Hardy, Kevin	Notre Dame U.	Richter, Pat	U. of Wisconsin
Calcavanti, Art	Bucknell U.	Holland (Brud) Jerome	Cornell U.	Robinson, Jackie	U. of Cal. at L.A.
Cassady, Hop-a-long	Ohio State U.	Huarte, John	Notre Dame U.	Sample, John	Maryland State
Collins, Gary	U. of Maryland	Johnson, Rafer	U. of Cal. at L.A.	Slater, Duke	U. of Iowa
Cornish, Frank	Grambling College	Jones, Calvin	U. of Iowa	Staubach, Roger	U. S. Naval Acad.
		Jones, Clinton	Michigan State	Stephens, Sandy	U. of Minnesota
		Kowalczyk, Walt	Michigan State	Tyler, Ralph	Livingstone College
		Lanier, Willie	Morgan State	Williams, J. T.	Oklahoma A&M
		Little, Floyd	Syracuse U.	Young, Buddy	U. of Illinois
		McLuckie, Tom	U. of Maryland	Young, Henry	Alabama A&M

Professional Baseball

Mays, Willie
Wills, Maury

NATIONAL INTERCOLLEGIATE FOOTBALL COACHES AND ATHLETIC DIRECTORS HONORED BY THE PIGSKIN CLUB OF WASHINGTON

Name	College	Name	College	Name	College
Bruhn, Milt	U. of Wisconsin	Hayes, Woody	Ohio State	Piggot, Bert	N. Carolina A&T College
Daugherty, Hugh	Michigan State	Jackson, Eddie	Delaware State	Schwartzwalder, Floyd	Syracuse U.
Devaney, Robert	U. of Nebraska	Hurt, Eddie	Morgan State	Robinson, Edward	Grambling College
Engle, Clyde	Pennsylvania State	McCain, Vernon	Maryland State	Tatem, Jim	U. of Maryland
Evashevski, Forest	U. of Iowa	Nicks, Bill	Prairie View	Wilson, Brutus	Shaw University
Gaither, Jake	Florida A&M	Parseghian, Ara	Notre Dame U.		

December 9, 1967

The Honorable Edward M Kennedy, the Honorable Edward Brook, Honorable Birch Bayh and the Honorable Hubert H. Humphrey attended the Pigskin Club in Washington, DC when I was honored as a Major National Intercollegiate Winner with Leroy Keyes, Purdue University; Granville Liggins, University of Oklahoma; John Pont, Indiana University.

Giving Back

Protégé Carlos Pena said I'm demanding, but also motivating—
he didn't mind the work.

Carlos Pena played 1st Base for Tampa

Johnson: He stresses a good attitude

Continued from Page 25

jumping rope and a distance run.

"The two things that are musts are the 'seated fast arms' (sitting on the ground and pumping arms furiously) and jump roping," said Johnson, who works in the window treatment business with his wife when not helping youngsters. "Other things are trial and error and depend on who I'm working with.

"One of the most important things is balance. Unless you have good balance, you can't run or compete effectively.

"It's hard work, but it can be done. My motto is, 'no deposit, no return.' If you make the right deposit, you'll get something out of it."

Anyone who has seen Pena play in college has seen his improvement in speed, but it's also been documented. At a New York Mets tryout more than a year ago, he was timed in 7.4 for 60 yards. Recently, Johnson timed him in 6.6 for the same distance.

Another of Johnson's students, 6-foot-4, 300-pound lineman Joel Gray of Haverhill has enjoyed even more improvement. An overweight (330), often-injured lineman at Haverhill High, Gray was timed in a crawling 6.5 for 40 yards back in 1994.

But, since that time, Gray has been working with Johnson and recently, while playing a post-grad year at Bridgton Academy in Maine, he was timed in 5.35.

"Daryl knows what you need and his positive reinforcement is unbelievable," said Gray. "My confidence level is 200 percent above what it used to be and I owe just about everything to Daryl."

And it shows. Gray played only five games in his total career at Haverhill, but he's already being noticed by large colleges while at Bridgton.

In his first two games this fall, against the Plymouth State and Yale JV teams, he had three sacks and made 13 tackles from his defensive tackle spot while also blocking two field goals and recovering a fumble.

What does Johnson get out of it? It's certainly not rewarding financially, since he offers his services for free.

"Part of it is ego, to prove people wrong," says Johnson. "I don't like people to say I can't coach because I know I can. And I don't like people who say you can't get faster.

"The other thing is self-satisfaction. I'm a result person. I like to see things grow. I like to plant flowers for that reason."

The Eagle Tribune, Oct. 2, 1997

The MBA Academy of Daryl Johnson
<u>M</u>ind <u>B</u>ody and <u>A</u>ttitude

John Mackey played for Baltimore Colts and San Diego Chargers. He was the first president of the NFL Players Association following the merger of the AFL-NFL serving from 1970-1973. A five-time Pro Bowler, Mackey was inducted into the Pro Football Hall of Fame in 1992. We worked together on the New England Minority Purchasing Council, Inc.

Volunteering to answer phones for a
PBA Telethon *before* area codes in Massachusetts

My wife, Helen, and Massachusetts State Auditor, Joe DeNucci

I was head coach of Track for Saugus High in Saugus, Massachusetts

Saugus High Track Team recognized my hard work and dedication.

Coach Daryl watching his Track Team at Saugus High.

The Greatest Coach We Know!

My 1983 Birthday Celebration

L-R Charlie Long-Patriots, Patrick Sullivan-owner's son, Bob Lobell-CBS Sports Anchorman, Antoine Patriots-Houston, and Jim Nance-Patriots

A positive attitude leads to happiness and success and can change your whole life

Giving Back and Paying Forward

Paying it forward involves doing something good for others in response to a good deed done on your behalf or a gift you received. This concept was popularized by a 2000 movie Pay It Forward. An important thing to remember is it should be done with a selfless spirit. This means it should be done without hoping for repayment or something in return.

Things to help you keep a positive attitude can be keeping a gratitude journal. Know there are no dead ends, only redirections. Get good at being rejected; when there are cracks in your heart, they let the sun in. Use positive words to describe your life. Replace have with get. Don't get dragged into other's peoples' complaints and understand the importance of taking a deep breath. Offer a solution when pointing out a problem and always make someone else smile.

1985 Textron Batting Champion Monogramed –
Daryl Johnson .479

Inspirational Sports Quotes

- "I hated every minute of training, but I said *don't quit, suffer now and live the rest of your life a champion. Champions aren't made in the gyms. Champions are made from something they have deep inside them, a desire, a dream, a vision.* " – Muhammad Ali, professional boxer
- "If you don't play well, you have a bad game or nightmare; you know that the amount of coverage is worldwide." – Steve Gerrard, Former Liverpool football captain
- "Luck has nothing to do with it, because I have spent many, many hours, countless hours, on the court working for my one moment in time, not knowing when it would come." Serena Williams
- "Success is no accident. It is hard work, perseverance, learning, studying, sacrifice and most of all, love of what you are doing or learning to do." – Pele, retired Brazilian footballer

RACE RELATIONS

While working for a big corporation, I attended their sports banquet. My boss' girlfriend and her friends presented a skit. She was pretending to be pregnant and her friends helped her to deliver the baby. They pulled out a Black Cabbage Patch Doll! I was the only Black person at the banquet and the only Black person in management. I was embarrassed and shocked because I was being honored. At the end they presented me with an ANRI WOOD CARVING TOKEN AWARD. It was a Black man wearing shoulder strap jeans, a straw hat, and he had gapped teeth. He was carrying a bail of cotton. Some folks laughed and a few told me they felt my pain that night.

Today's racial climate continues to require us to be strong, get involved in community activities and VOTE. Be aware that some racism will always exist.

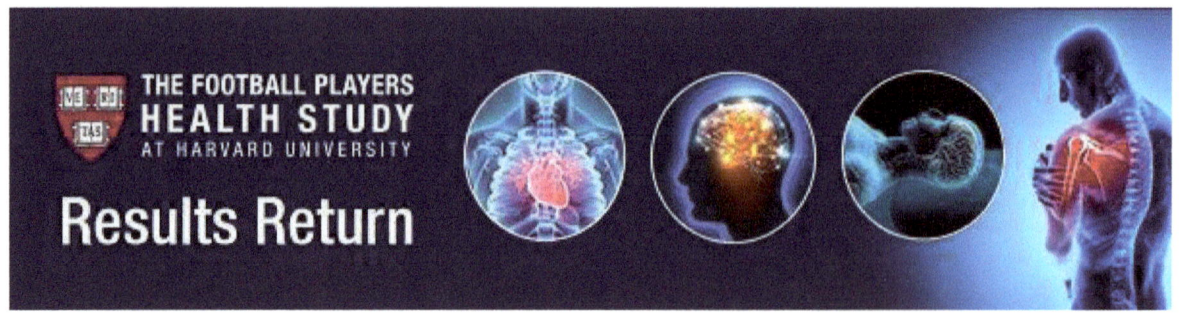

Harvard University Health Study

Dear Mr. Johnson,

One of our Study's priorities is to better understand the health impacts of concussion. Another is to identify how particular NFL playing experiences affect health outcomes. The findings below shed light on both of these topics, showing how concussions, NFL career length and playing position may impact your long-term cognitive and mental health. You will also find some action steps and resources to help you be proactive about these aspects of your health.

What the Science Says

Our analysis of 3,500 former NFL players looked at individuals' current cognitive and mental health alongside the specific exposures they encountered during their NFL careers, using the health and playing data that former players reported on themselves in our First Health and Wellness questionnaire (Q1). Here's what we found:

Concussion Symptoms: Former players who reported more concussion symptoms during their NFL playing years (loss of consciousness, disorientation, nausea, etc.) were significantly more likely to report having cognitive impairment[1], depression and anxiety later in life.

Playing Position: In comparison to men who played positions with the lowest concussion risk (kicker, punter and quarterback), running backs, linebackers and special teams[2] positions were over twice as likely to report having cognitive impairment and 40% more likely to report depression. Wide receivers, defensive backs, linemen and tight ends were 70% more likely to report cognitive impairment and 40% more likely to report depression when compared to the lowest risk group.

Harvard Letter (continued)

Years of Play: Having a longer NFL career significantly increased risk of cognitive impairment and depression later in life. With each 5 years of play, risk for cognitive impairment increased by 20%, while risk for depression rose by 9%.

[1] In this study, cognitive impairment was defined as frequent and regular problems with memory, concentration, and attention, as well as difficulty processing and understanding basic information.

[2] This group includes all special teams' positions except for kickers and punters. Kickers and punters were assessed as a separate group, alongside quarterbacks.

This is the first large-scale study to quantify the specific risks associated with NFL career length and playing position, and an important step in beginning to understand how playing exposures may impact health. However, more research is needed on this topic before any definitive conclusions can be drawn. Additionally, it is important to understand that there are a number of different variables that affect cognitive health, and that many individuals who had the playing exposures outlined above will not experience cognitive impairment or poor mental health. As the graph below illustrates, even among those players who experienced the highest levels of exposure (i.e., individuals who played for 7 seasons or more in high-risk positions), the percentage of men who reported cognitive impairment did not exceed 16%.

The Greatest Wealth is Health

Health Notes

Fifty years ago, the NFL didn't have a concussion protocol. They would just tell you to "be a man and shake it off." I can remember having a serious headache after every pro game I played. One game was against the Miami Dolphins in Miami. I tackled a guy by the name of Larry Csonka, and I did not wake up until the team plane landed at Logan Airport in Boston. That scared me. But the team doctor said no big deal. Of course, you are going to trust the doctor.

So from that game on, I had trouble with my head and sight. I did feel my personality was changing. Thank God I broke my leg. It caused me to have to sit out a season. It gave me an opportunity to find me again. This Harvard study is for all of us former players. I'm not donating my brain after I die; I'm taking my brain with me.

Injuries I suffered for the love of football: I had eleven plus concussions, one subdural hematoma when I was playing for the Houston Texans of the World Football League. I dislocated both shoulders, broken leg that required a hip cast, dislocated fingers on both hands. I did not suffer with depression, I'm still alive, I have nothing to be depressed about. It's like you are taught in football…next play. In the game of life, it's the next day. I'm not suggesting everyone should think that way… I'm suggesting they should try.

I play golf on beautifully manicured courses. The luscious greens and fragrant flowers put my mind in a peaceful competitive state.

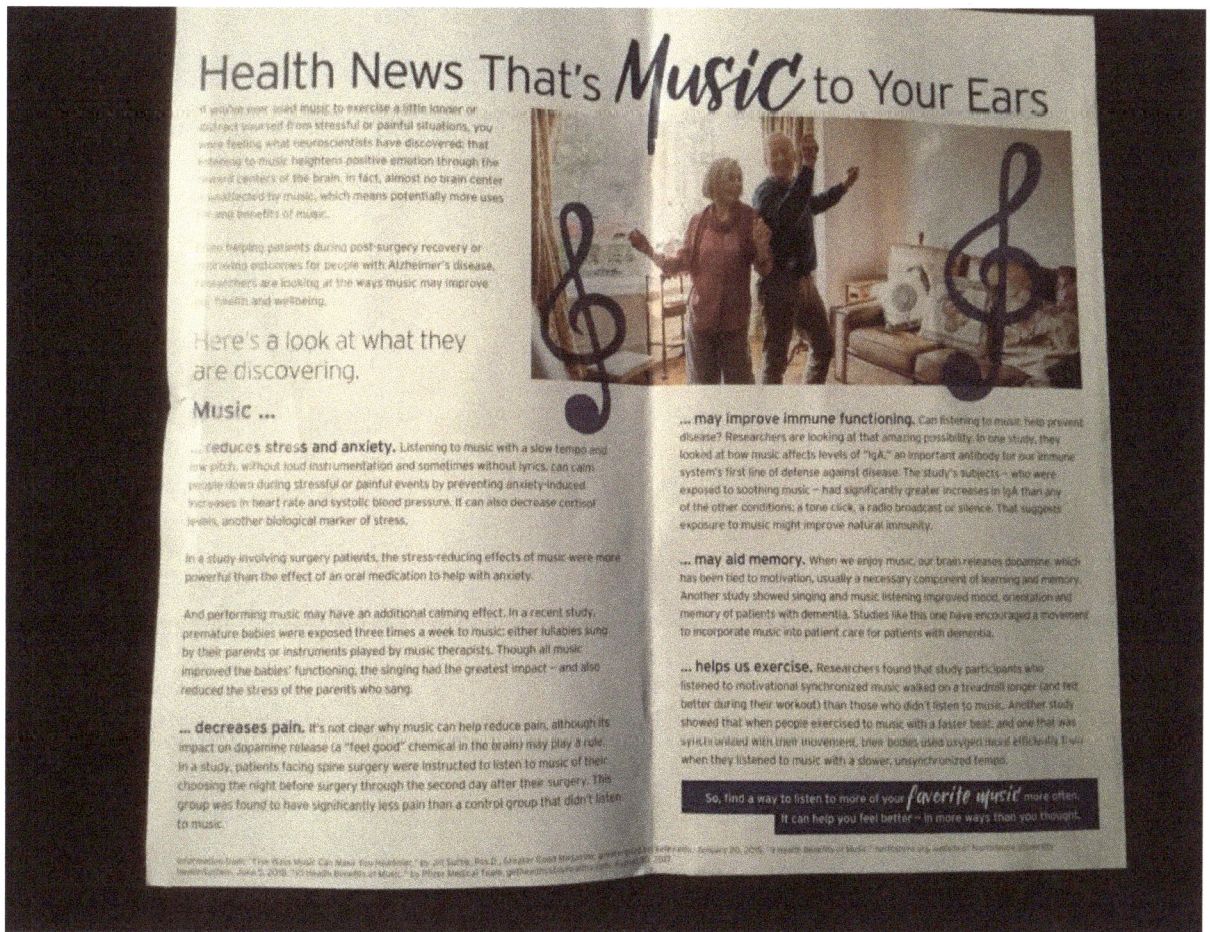

Physicians Mutual Conversations Between Friends — January 2019

I love Music. Studies have shown if you want to transform your mood, *cue the music*! It can improve your well-being, reduce stress and decrease pain. It may also improve your memory and your immune system. On *YouTube*, my daughter, Brandi Johnson, has started a playlist— *Dr. T Inspirational Music*, check it out.

A BRIEF WORD ABOUT COVID-19

We are making major adjustments to our lives during this pandemic. Quarantines have been imposed, trade has been restricted and activities and public gatherings have been limited.

Folks in my age group and younger have never experienced anything like this. Helen allows me to venture out three days a week and that's only to go to the Palace, as I call it, to get my blood washed!

As the music pumps in my earbuds, I reflect on my supportive family and friends ... I think and take stock of my life and I am pleased to share it with you in this book. The letters, awards, newspaper articles, and photographs tell an accurate story. Some roads were bumpy and some turns may not have been the best but my family and friends tell me, "A job well done!" My teammates called me Dr. T. They said it was for Dr. Touchdown. I am extremely humble and smiled within.

My advice to the young athlete is...life is a game and the obstacles with people are a result of our differences. Look for the positive, stop judging yourself and others; focus on the NOW. Get your education and listen to your coaches. Keep a positive mental attitude. If it's the PRO LIFE you want you must be *mentally and physically strong* and keep that burning desire to be the BEST. Make smart choices, build healthy relationships and don't forget to give back to your community.

During the Pandemic of 2020 the doctors and nurses at the Palace asked me how I remained so calm and stylish during this perilous time ...I replied, "That's what I do."

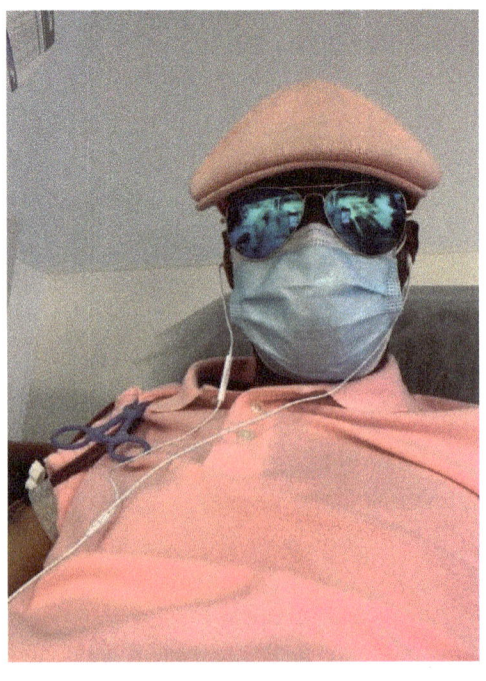 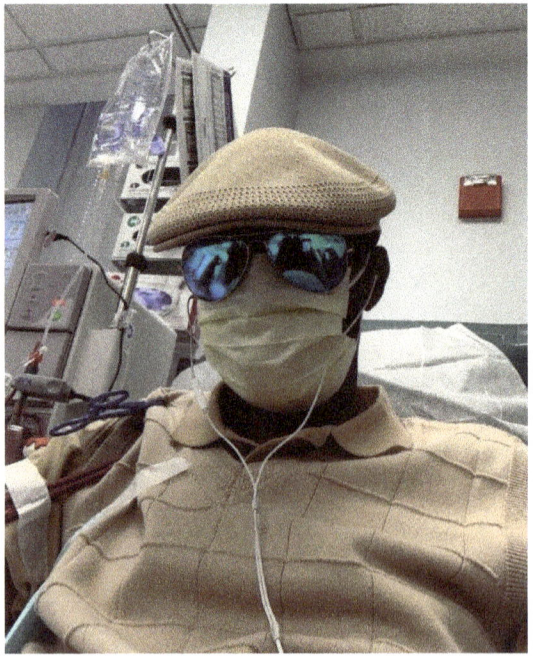

Inspirational Sports Quotes

- "Money does not guarantee success." – Jose Mourinho, manager of Manchester United FC)
- "Behind every kick of the ball there has to be a thought." – Dennis Bergkamp, former Dutch player
- "Fail to prepare, prepare to fail." – Roy Keane, former captain of both Manchester United and Ireland
- "Every single day I wake up and commit to myself to becoming a better player." – Mia Hamm, retired soccer player
- If I feel I'm not influencing games, not scoring goals or making goals, then that's the time I'd pack it in." Ryan Giggs, former captain of Wales
- "Losing is not in my vocabulary." – Ruud van Nistelrooy, retired Dutch footballer
- "When I was younger I was trying to do what I wanted to do, not what the game wanted me to do." – Thierry Henry, retired French footballer
- "I never dreamed about being a millionaire, I dreamed about being a football player." – Victor Cruz, NFL football player New York Giants
- "I learned that the only way you are going to get anywhere in life is to work hard at it. Whether you're a musician, a writer, an athlete or a businessman, there is no getting around it. If you do, you win—if you don't, you won't" – Bruce Jenner, Decathlon Olympic Gold Medalist
- "The highest compliment that you can pay me is to say that I work hard every day, that I never dog it." – Wayne Gretzsky, Canadian Hockey Player
- "To uncover your true potential, you must first find your own limits and then you have to have the courage to blow past them." – Picabo Street, World Cup Alpine Olympic Gold Medalist
- "The price of success is hard work, dedication to the job at hand, and the determination that whatever we win or lose, we have applied the best of ourselves to the task at hand." Vince Lombardi

Catching Up With ... Ex-Morgan State QB Daryl Johnson, who played for Patriots

By **Mike Klingaman**

The Baltimore Sun

Jan 09, 2015 | 8:58 AM

Morgan State quarterback Daryl Johnson hands off to Earl Mayo during a game in 1966. (Paul Hutchins, Baltimore Sun)

Sometimes, looking back, Daryl Johnson wonders if it truly happened. Did he really lead Morgan State's football team to two undefeated seasons and then play in the pros for the Patriots?

"It's a life you dream about as a kid. Then, while you're living it, you can't believe it," said Johnson, 68, of Haverhill, Mass. "And now, while watching the Ravens play New England [Saturday], I'll be thinking, 'Was that actually me out there years ago?

An eighth-round draft pick of the then-Boston Patriots in 1968, Johnson was a three-year starter at defensive back before a broken leg ended his NFL career. But it was in college where he left his mark, starring at quarterback and shattering Morgan's passing records during the Bears' 31- game unbeaten streak in the mid-1960s.

Then, Morgan was a black college powerhouse, routinely outscoring opponents by four or five touchdowns and landing 18 players in the pros.

Johnson played alongside Hall of Famer Willie Lanier (Kansas City Chiefs), Frenchy Fuqua (Pittsburgh Steelers), Raymond Chester (Baltimore Colts), Mark Washington (Dallas Cowboys), George Nock (New York Jets) and Carlton Dabney (Atlanta Falcons).

"For them to just sit and watch inspired us," Johnson said. "We thought we were damn good but the only way to prove it was to *be* damn good."

In 1965 — Johnson's sophomore season — Morgan won all eight games, six by shutouts, as the Bears outscored their rivals 265-27.

"Coach [Earl] Banks said, 'The best way to win is not to let the other team score.' That made sense to us," he said.

Banks, aka "Poppa Bear," allowed no grandstanding, Johnson said:

"If you showed off after making a tackle or knocking down a pass, you'd go back to your locker and find a bottle of French's mustard and a package of hot dogs."

A 5-foot-10, 175-pound walk-on from Richmond, Va., Johnson played wide receiver and place kicker before moving to quarterback as a junior. Again, the Bears went unbeaten, averaged 40 points and finished with a 14-6 victory over West Chester State (Pa.) in the Tangerine Bowl in Orlando. That game, in 1966, celebrated the first postseason win by a historically black college against a predominately white one.

"Back then, black college teams were considered a little better than high school," Johnson said. "But we thought we could play with anyone in the country, so we sure weren't going to let them [West Chester] beat us." Or anyone else, on Johnson's watch. His senior year, the Bears went 8-0 and were invited back to the Tangerine Bowl. But the players nixed the bid upon learning they'd face West Chester again.

"A bunch of the guys felt they had nothing to prove," he said. "Me? I was ready to beat them twice."

Maryland College Team, he completed 54 percent of his passes for 1,050 yards, a school record. He ran for six touchdowns and converted 27 of 33 extra points. The Pigskin Club of Washington, D.C. honored him as NCAA Small College Player of the Year.

"Our [offensive] line was outstanding. I was hardly ever sacked," he said.

"Whenever we played in the rain, I'd always jump in the mud so people wouldn't think I hadn't played."

Most important, Johnson left with Morgan's 26-game winning streak intact.

"Coach always told us, 'Don't be the team that breaks the streak.' So everyone was relieved when they graduated," he said.

Boston proved different. In Johnson's three years there, the Patriots won 10 of 42 games.

"At Morgan, I remember looking across the field and wondering how it felt to be losing, 40-0," he said. "I found out, playing for Boston."

Johnson tried to psyche up the Patriots. "I dyed my football shoes red, but the league wouldn't allow it," he said. And he shared poems with the media before each game, to wit:

"With [Miami receiver Paul] Warfield out there, we'll be under the gun, But I still think I'm going to hold him to one."

After football, Johnson worked in auto sales, as a stockbroker and as an insurance claims adjuster before retiring. Married 30 years, he has two children, one grandchild and an interest in latch hooking (wall hangings made of acrylic yarns). A kidney ailment requires dialysis three times a week.

"I had about seven concussions in football, so I keep testing myself to see if I'm still sane," he said. "I come up with a 50-50 response because, honestly, you have to be crazy to play the game in the first place." *mike.klingaman@baltsun.com*

Links

Dr. T's Uplifting Playlist on YouTube by Brandi Johnson

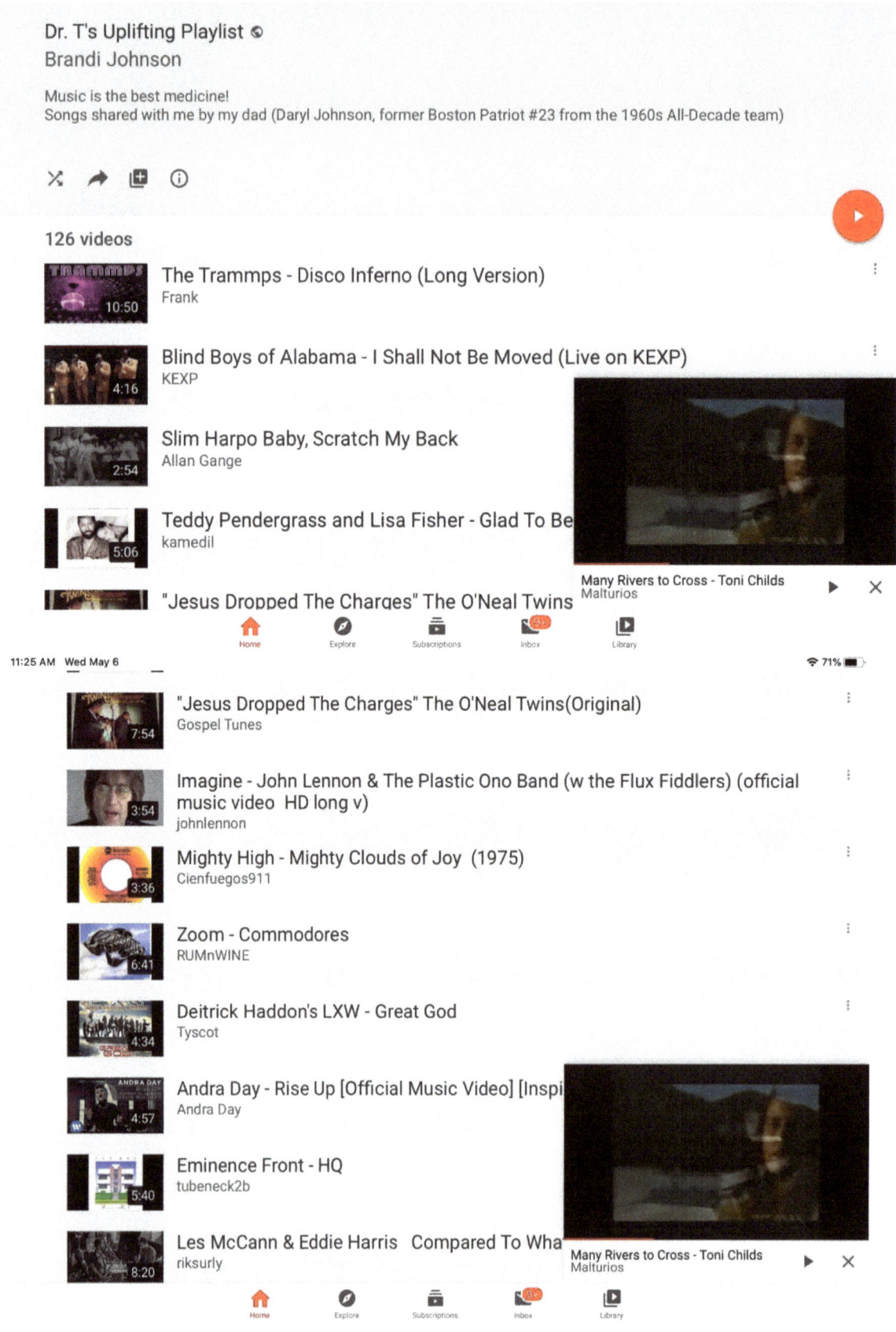

11:25 AM Wed May 6   71%

Tom Petty And The Heartbreakers - I Won't Back Down (Official Music Video)
tompetty
3:02

George Benson - Six to Four
60otaku4
5:15

Lakeside - Fantastic Voyage
sazhawk
6:14

Funkadelic-(Not Just) Knee Deep
Nervioso_xD
5:10

Patti LaBelle - New Attitude (Official Music Video)
Patti Labelle Fan
4:04

The O'Jays - Love Train
TOP 40 1973
3:03

One Nation Under A Groove - Funkadelic (1978)
1mistaGROOVE
7:24

Hamilton Bohannon   Foot Stompin Music   197
Mickyp60
7:12

Many Rivers to Cross - Toni Childs
Malturios

11:25 AM Wed May 6   70%

McFadden & Whitehead Ain't No Stopping Us Now (long Version).wmv
patricia du prée
10:47

Yardbrough & Peoples - Don't Stop The Music
BrownPrider Funk
7:47

Joe Tex - Ain't Gonna Bump No More {With No Big Fat Woman} (1977 Audio Redone By Dj Cole)
DjCole100
4:16

Sister Act 2 (Finale) Lauryn Hill - Joyful Joyful With Lyrics (Ft. Whoopi Goldberg)
Bound4Earth
4:29

Brothers Johnson - Get The Funk Out Ma Face
AuntieSoul34
6:03

WAKE UP EVERYBODY - Original Version (Teddy the Blue Notes)
yxyoic
7:34

Let's Work
Prince
3:55

Earth, Wind & Fire - That's the Way of the World
Earth Wind & Fire
5:48

Many Rivers to Cross - Toni Childs
Malturios

Home   Explore   Subscriptions   Inbox   Library

138

Zoom: The Playing Field of Daryl E. Johnson

2Pac - Changes ft. Talent
2Pac

50 Cent - In Da Club (Int'l Version) [Official Video]
50 Cent

Hamilton Bohannon - Let's Start The Dance (Original 12 Inch V)
VinsentDj

Kool & The Gang - Celebration (Official Video)
KoolandthegangShow

Sheila E - A Love Bizarre (Album Version) (HD)
Dr. SuperFunk

Bill Withers ~ Lovely Day 1977 Disco Purrfection
DJDiscoCatV2

JUNIOR - Mama Used To Say
TokyoPopCity

It's All The Way Live(1978)
Dantoine93

Many Rivers to Cross - Toni Childs
Malturios

Frankie Smith - Double Dutch Bus (Official Music Video)
UnidiscMusic

Kool & The Gang - Tonight
tifosicalcio

Can You Feel It
The Jacksons - Topic

Kool & The Gang - Let's Go Dancing (Ooh, La, La, La) (Official Music Video)
KoolandthegangShow

Fleetwood Mac - Gypsy (Official Music Video)
Fleetwood Mac

Kirk Franklin - I Smile (Official Video)
Kirk Franklin

Brothers Johnson "Tomorrow" Quincy Jones 1
mosogotam

Kirk Franklin-Stomp Featuring Salt
marslover5

Many Rivers to Cross - Toni Childs
Malturios

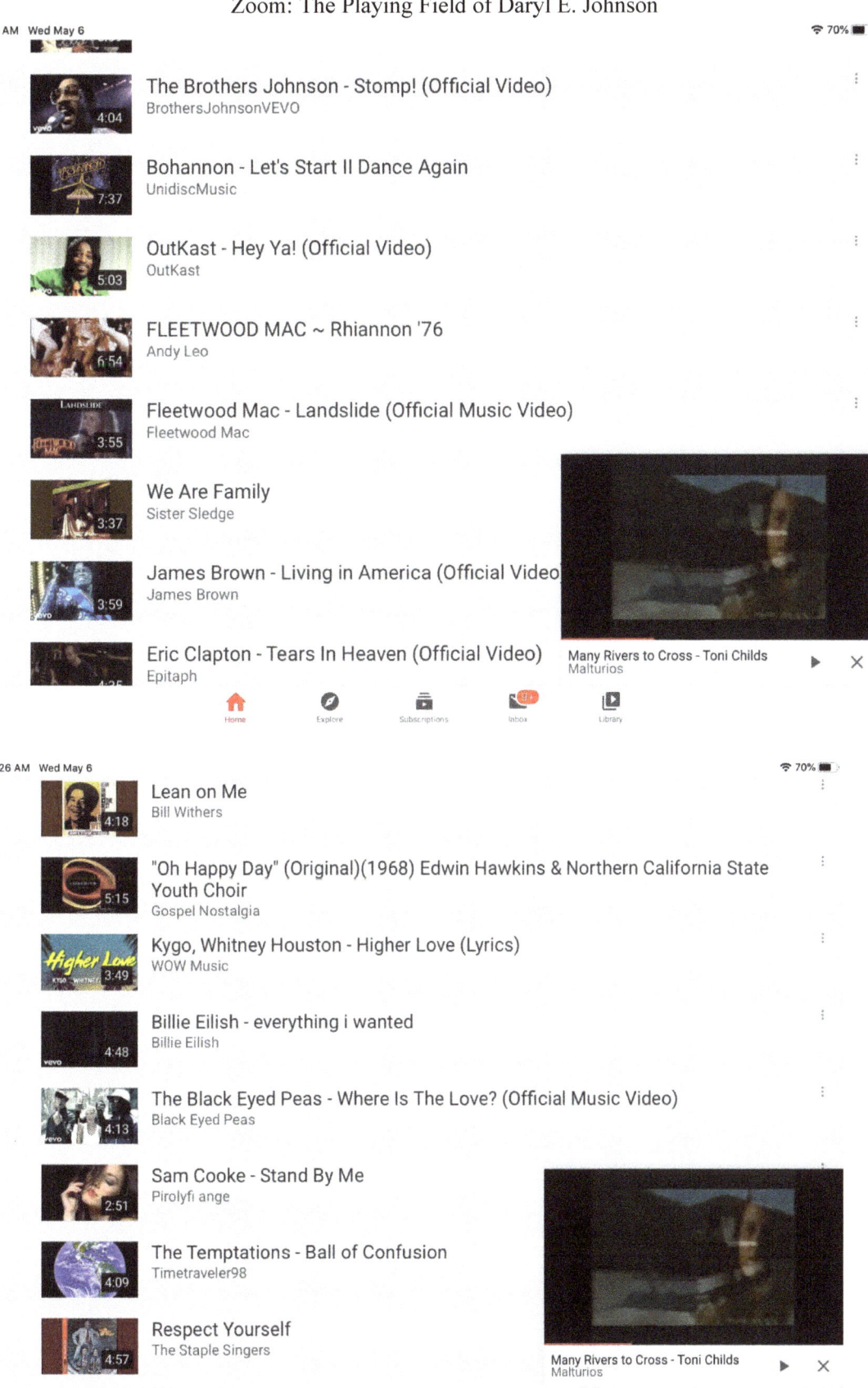

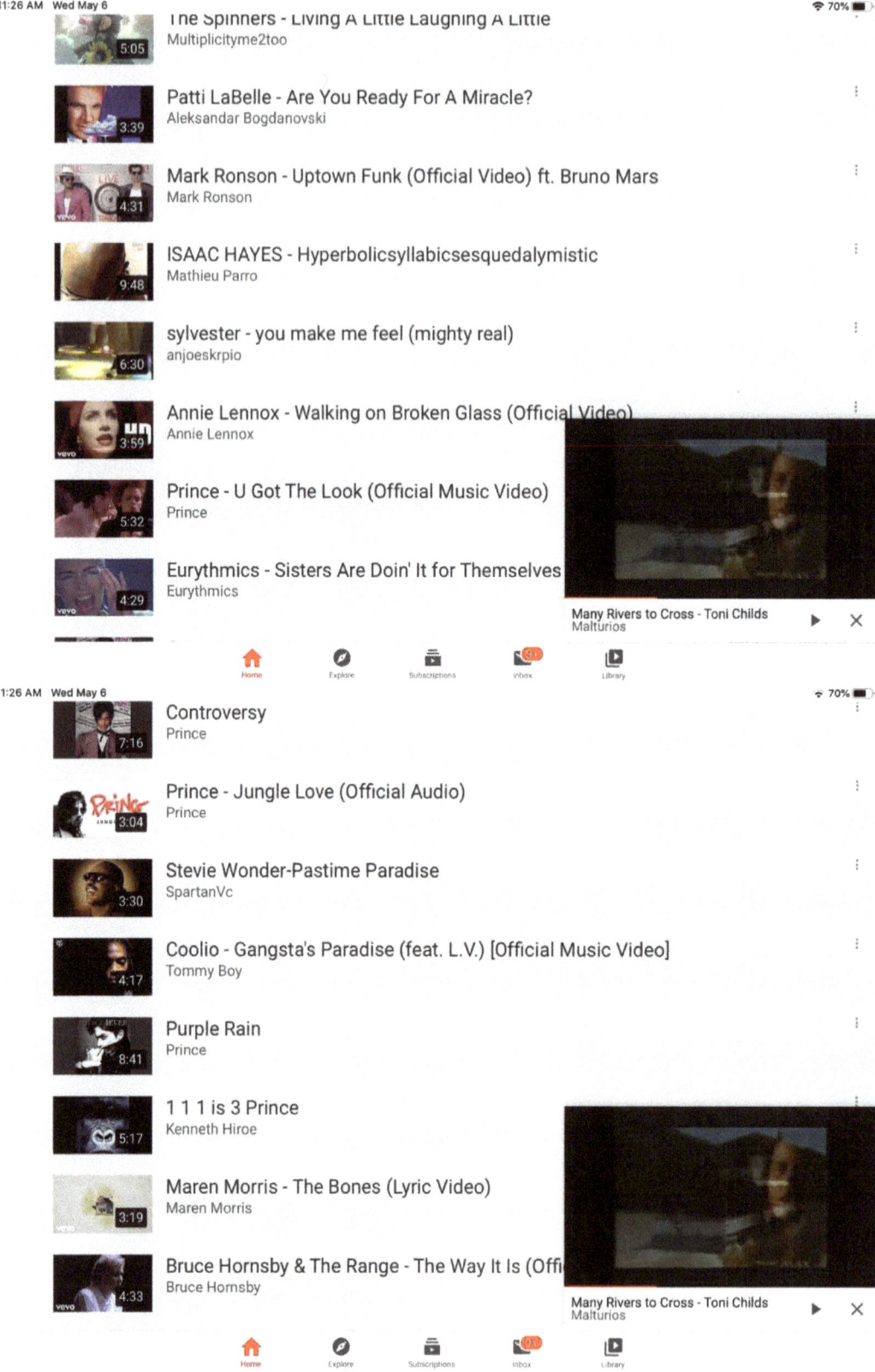

Zoom: The Playing Field of Daryl E. Johnson

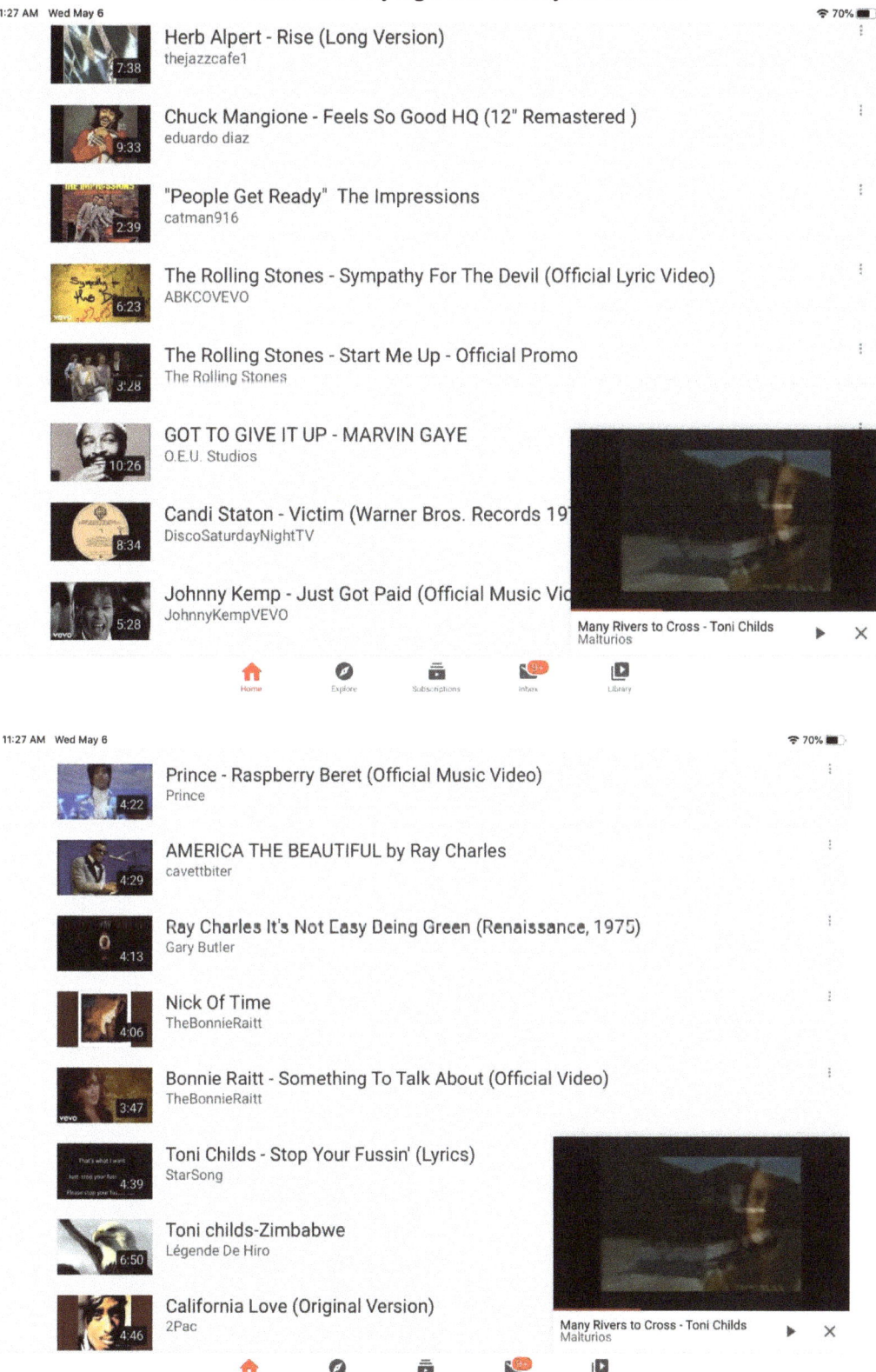

142   Zoom: The Playing Field of Daryl E. Johnson

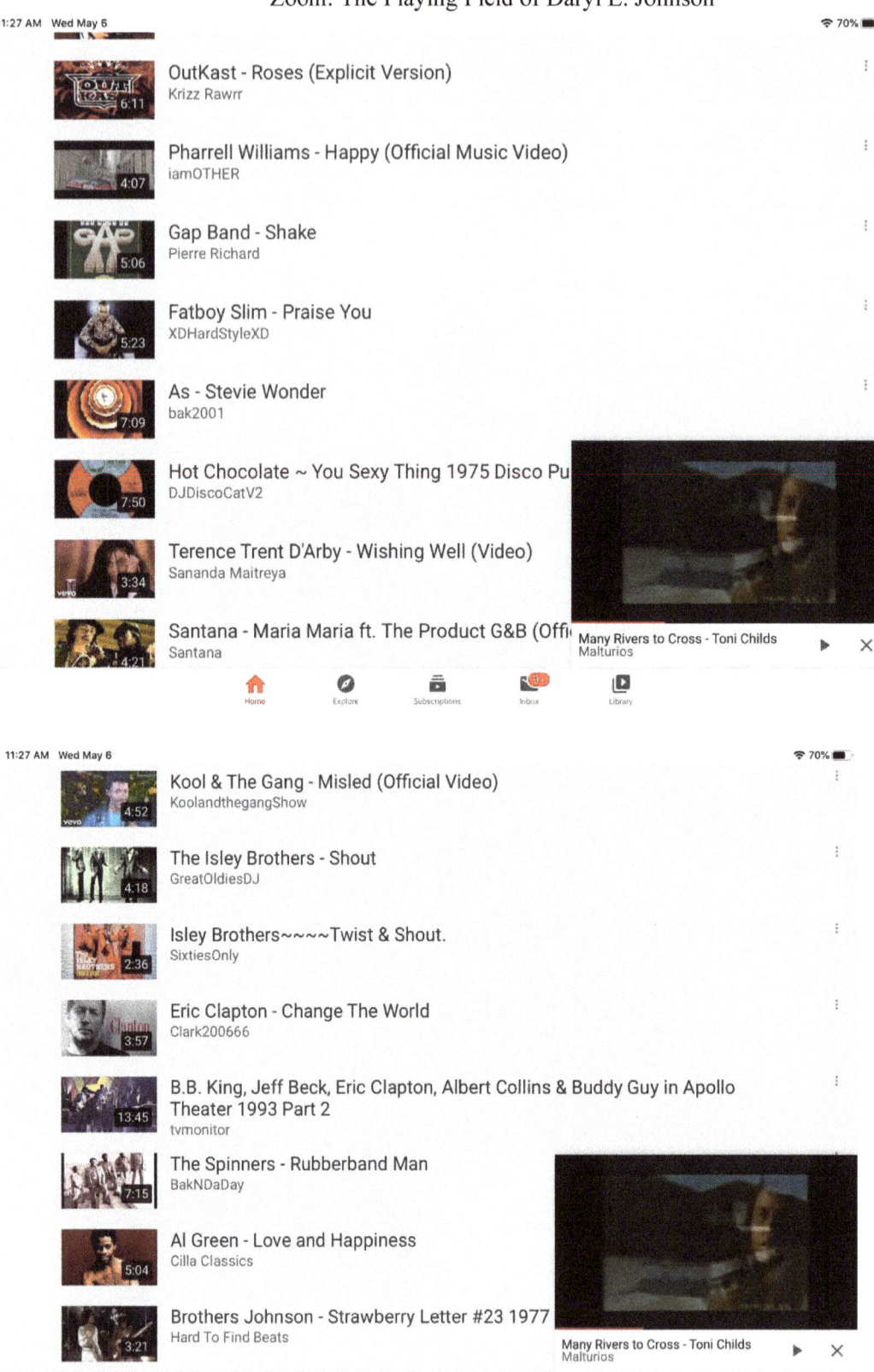

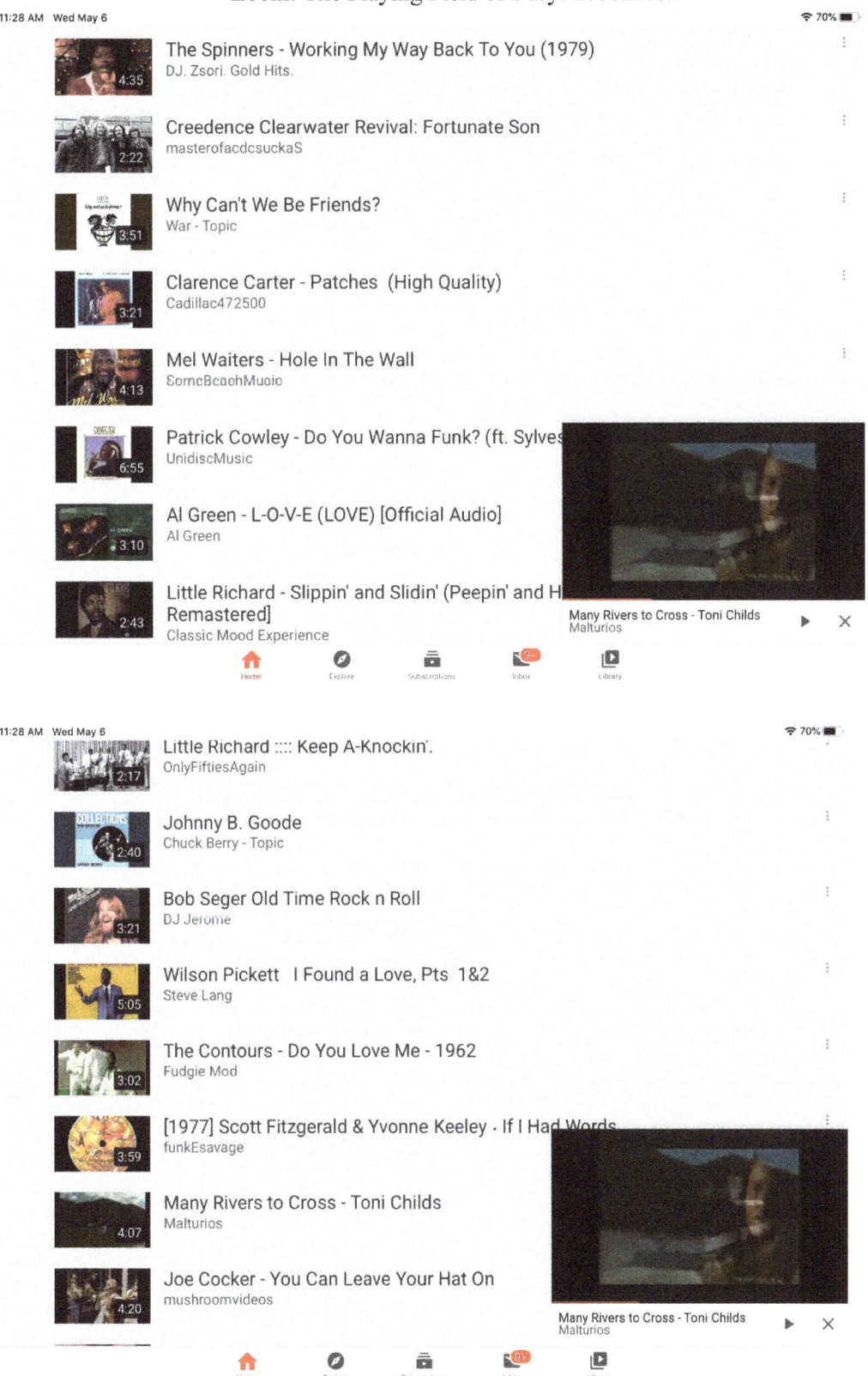

Robert Palmer - Simply Irresistible (Official Video)
Parlophone Records

Stevie Nicks - Edge of Seventeen (Official Music Video)
Stevie Nicks

Otis Redding - A Change Is Gonna Come
Superbrownybear

Joe Cocker - She Came In Through The Bathroom Window (Live)
Joe Cocker Official

Daryl E. Johnson
From Wikipedia, the free encyclopedia

Daryl E. Johnson (born August 11, 1946) is a former American football defensive back who played in the American Football League, the National Football League, and the World Football League.

College career

Johnson graduated from Maggie L. Walker High School in Richmond. He entered Morgan State University in 1964 and received his Bachelor of Science in Business Administration degree. Mr. Johnson (5'10½"/170 lbs), was an invited walk-on at Morgan State, where he became a four-year letterman in football playing on three undefeated CIAA Championship football teams from 1965–1967, and was a two-year letterman in track and field.

Mr. Johnson acquired many honors during his amazing college football career: however, he carved his own piece of Morgan State athletic history as the starting quarterback during the undefeated 1966 and 1967 CIAA Championship football seasons. In 1966, Morgan State University became the first predominately African American team selected to play in the NCAA sanctioned Tangerine Bowl (now called the Capital One Bowl). Mr. Johnson led the Morgan State Golden Bears on one of the biggest stages the University had been on to a historic 14-6 victory over West Chester State (PA). The victory earned Morgan State University the distinction of being crowned the first historically black college or university (HBCU) to win a nationally recognized NCAA Championship Title, Atlantic Coast Champions. Mr. Johnson ended the 1966 season being selected to the first-team Maryland All-State Team as a Placekicker and first-team ALL-CIAA.

During the 1967 season, Daryl led the Golden Bears to their third consecutive CIAA Championship and undefeated seasons. He set a school record by becoming the first quarterback to pass for over 1,000 yards in a single season, completing 54 percent of his passes for 1,050 yards. His senior year performance was so outstanding that he was selected first Team Maryland All-State as Quarterback, first Team All-CIAA Quarterback and first Team *Pittsburgh Courier* Black All-American Defensive Back.

Daryl finished his career leading Morgan State to the longest winning streak in college football at the time. The Golden Bears only lost two games during Mr. Johnson's four-year career. While playing for Morgan, Daryl played quarterback, flanker, defensive back and was the teams placekicker.

Johnson is a member of Morgan State University's Varsity "M" Club athletic Hall Of Fame.

Professional career[edit]

Johnson was selected 1968 Common Draft in the 8th round. He would play for the American Football League's Boston Patriots (1968–1969), the National Football League's Boston Patriots (1970). Johnson became a starter in his rookie season. He was selected to the Boston Patriots All-Time Team of the Decades of the 1960s and honored at a special pre-game and halftime ceremony on December 5, 1971 at Schaefer in conjunction with Gino Cappelletti Day. Daryl was also a starting defensive back in the World Football League with the Houston Texans/Shreveport Steamers.

Personal

Johnson is married to Helen Griffin, and they have two children, Deron and Brandi, as well as one granddaughter, Nevaeh.

Inspirational Sports Quotes

- "For *sportsmen and women* who want to be champions, the mind can be as important, if not most important, than any other part of the body." – Gary Neville, former England and Manchester United footballer

- "A lot of football success is in the mind, you must believe you are the best and then make sure that you are" – Bill Shankly, Scottish Football Manager

- "You have to perform at a consistently higher level than others. That's the mark of a true professional." – Joe Paterno, Former football coach

- "Before you can win, you have to believe you are worthy," – Mike Ditka, former football NFL player, television commentator, and coach

Remember, it's not the game you play, *more importantly*, it's how you play the game.

- "To succeed…you need to find something to hold on to, something to motivate you, something to inspire you." – Tony Dorsett, football champion

When you contemplate the hat you will wear in life, wear it with *distinction*.

You will often find me in sunglasses, caps and hats. Hats are artful and if you *tilt your hat a bit* it signals a good attitude. Hats are all about emotion...how they make you feel. I'm not trying to avoid anyone with my shades, I'm just being me! I lived during the era of Black Pride, "express yo-self," so bright colors have always been a part of my wardrobe.

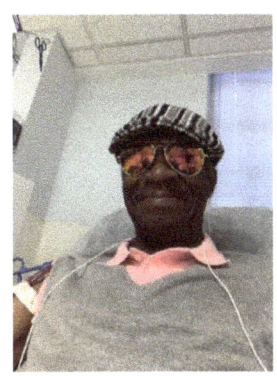

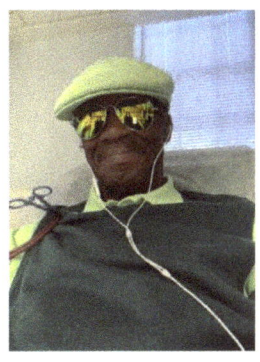

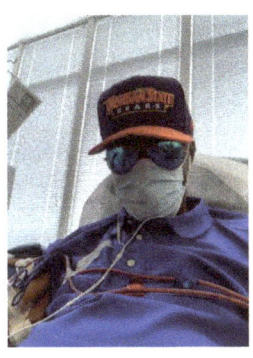

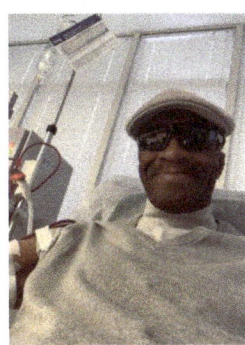
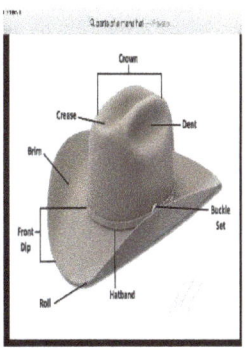

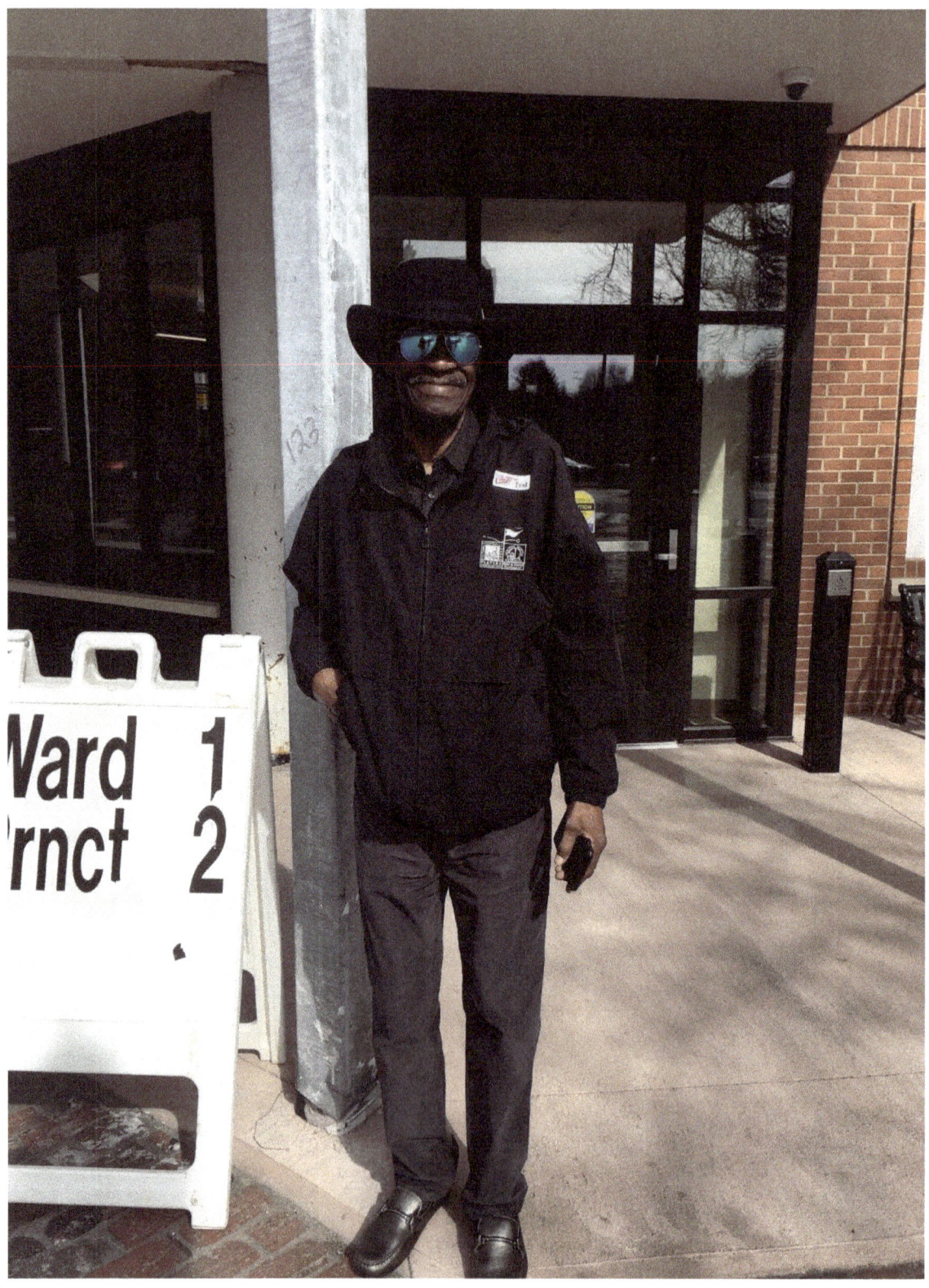

Daryl Says, *VOTE!*

About the Author

Gayle Jones Carter is Vice President of DeVoreCarter Communications, a continuation of the Ophelia DeVore philosophy and training as it relates to personal and professional development. Ophelia DeVore is the author's mother-in-law. Gayle has many awards Including the City of New York African American Business Award and Outstanding Women of the World Award.

The mission of DeVoreCarter Communications is to guide clients, individuals and corporations, to strengthen their personal presentation through enhanced development and training.

Gayle and Daryl grew up together on the Northside of Richmond, VA attending the same schools from elementary through high school.

Gayle was unaware of Daryl's big dreams and unwavering drive to achieve them. Zoom reveals to the reader a prospective of Daryl's life in pictures and conversations "accumulated" only by the author via electronic media.

Daryl's perseverance is a direct result of his refusal to be stopped by any hurdles life throws his way.

QR Code Links

Scan Codes with Your Phone Camera

Internet Search (type): Daryl E. Johnson NFL Clip (Boston Patriots)
NFL VIDEO OF DARYL:
Link 2 min 53 sec:

Internet (type):
https://drive.google.com/file/d/16aME55QTGUYapaQfn8PUYhCWtGXg6uXC/view
Daryl's Radio Show Link:
Your Sports IQ: 53.24 minutes

ZOOM
Credits

Maggie L. Walker Yearbooks, 1964 and 1945
Richmond Afro American
The Baltimore Sun, Jan 9, 2015
Morgan State Football stats and photos
Belmont, MA Newspaper
Marcus McGee, Publisher, Pegasus Books
DeVoreCarter Communications, LLC
LaJuan Carter Dent
James Devore Carter
Harvard University Football Players Health Study
Physicians Mutual Conversations between Friends– January 2019
YouTube – Dr. T's Uplifting Playlist – Brandi Johnson
Eagle Tribune Newspaper
Boston Patriots Alumni Photos and Stats
NFL Video
Cover Design by Jerimiah Johnson
Back Cover Artist Rendering, Larry Johnson, Jr.
Wikipedia
Daryl E. Johnson
Helen Johnson
Brandi Johnson
Deron Johnson
Dr. Carolyn Brooks
Dr. Gregory E. Douglas